FASHION DESIGN

Anette Fischer and Kiran Gobin

UNIVERSITY OF
GLOUCESTERSHIRE
at Cheltenham and Gloucester

# Construction for Fashion Design

Second edition

**Bloomsbury Visual Arts**
An imprint of Bloomsbury Publishing Plc

B L O O M S B U R Y
LONDON · OXFORD · NEW YORK · NEW DELHI · SYDNEY

**Bloomsbury Visual Arts**

An imprint of Bloomsbury Publishing Plc

Imprint previously known as AVA Publishing

50 Bedford Square
London
WC1B 3DP
UK

1385 Broadway
New York
NY 10018
USA

**www.bloomsbury.com**

**BLOOMSBURY VISUAL ARTS, BLOOMSBURY and the Diana logo
are trademarks of Bloomsbury Publishing Plc**

First published by AVA Publishing SA, 2009
This 2nd edition is published by Bloomsbury Visual Arts, an imprint
of Bloomsbury Publishing Plc
Copyright © Bloomsbury Publishing Plc, 2017

**British Library Cataloguing-in-Publication Data**
A catalogue record for this book is available from the British Library.

ISBN:     PB:     978-1-4725-3875-8
ePDF:   978-1-4725-3876-5

**Library of Congress Cataloging-in-Publication Data**
Names: Fischer, Anette, Gobin, Kiran, author.
Title: Construction for fashion designer / Kiran Gobin.
Description: London, UK ; New York, NY, USA : Bloomsbury Visual Arts, [2017] |
Series: Basics fashion design | Includes bibliographical references and index.
Identifiers: LCCN 2016022178| ISBN 9781472538758 (pbk. : alk. paper) | ISBN
9781472538765 (ePDF)
Subjects: LCSH: Clothing trade. | Dressmaking. | Tailoring. | Garment cutting. | Sewing.
Classification: LCC TT497 .G63 2017 | DDC 646.4–dc23 LC record available at
https://lccn.loc.gov/2016022178
Series: Basics Fashion Design

Cover design: Louise Dugdale

Cover image: Amy Hector photography © Danny Kasirye

Typeset by Lachina

Printed and bound in China

To find out more about our authors and books visit www.bloomsbury.com.
Here you will find extracts, author interviews, details of forthcoming events
and the option to sign up for our newsletters.

0.1 Balenciaga AW16.

# Contents

# 5

## Haute couture and tailoring  109

# 6

## Draping on the mannequin  125

# 7

## Garment support and structure  141

# 8

## Finishes  175

> **"Do not quench your inspiration and your imagination; do not become the slave of your model."**
> Vincent Van Gogh

Construction is the foundation of clothing and of fashion design; it is vital that fashion designers know and understand the techniques involved in creating a three-dimensional garment from a two-dimensional design or pattern in order to create a beautiful shape and fit on a moving body. Garment construction involves both technical and design issues; the designer can choose where to construct lines, pockets, collars, how to finish edges and how to produce volume and structure in order to create a unique look and experience for the wearer.

From basic block cutting to the smallest finishing details on a constructed garment, *Basics Fashion Design: Construction for Fashion Design* leads you through the essential stages of garment construction and offers you a starting point from which knowledge can be extended. It introduces you to the world of pattern cutting, draping on the mannequin and shows you some techniques for breathing life into a flat design drawing in order to achieve a three-dimensional garment.

Basic sewing techniques are introduced, and you are shown how to use darts, sleeves, collars, pockets and the cut of the fabric to add variation to your designs. The breadth of the subject is illustrated with a history of garment shape and construction techniques in haute couture, tailoring crafts and an introduction to supporting and structuring materials. Each chapter also includes interviews from leading practitioners and tasks to help you understand these techniques. The book concludes with finishing techniques and a selection of resources for those wishing to delve deeper into the world of construction for fashion.

With its inspirational photography and easy-to-follow diagrams, *Construction for Fashion Design* offers a clear introduction to the fundamental skills, knowledge and historical background needed for successful garment construction. I hope it will awaken your interest and inspire you to create the perfect silhouette and a beautiful, final piece.

**0.2 Craig Green SS16**

# Getting Started

**1**

It is important for designers to understand the fundamentals of how a garment grows from a two-dimensional concept into a three-dimensional object. A pattern is a flat paper or card template from which the parts of the garment are transferred to fabric before being cut out and assembled.

A good understanding of body shape and how body measurements transfer to the pattern piece is essential. The pattern cutter must work accurately in order to ensure that, once constructed, the parts of the fabric fit together properly and precisely.

This chapter is an introduction to pattern cutting, starting with the tools and equipment needed. Then it takes a look at the processes involved: the importance of silhouettes and proportion; sizing and grading and how to take body measurements. Finally, it introduces the basic block and pattern shapes and how the body measurements relate to these.

**1.1 Roksanda Ilincic, AW15.**

# Pattern cutting tools and equipment

Working with the right tools will make block and pattern construction easier. These are just some of the key pieces of equipment required.

**Tailor's chalk (1)** Using tailor's chalk is one way of marking lines or transferring a pattern on to cloth.

**Set of three French curves (2)** These are used for drawing narrower curves, such as those found on collars and pockets.

**43 cm set square (3)** This is a right-angled triangular plate used for drawing lines, particularly at 90 degrees and 45 degrees.

**Wooden awl (4)** This is used for marking any points within the pattern piece by punching through the pattern to leave a small mark on the fabric.

**Pins (5)** These are used to temporarily fix pieces of paper or cloth together.

**Tape measure (6)** An indispensable item, this is used for taking measurements of the body and its flexibility allows curved lines to be measured, too.

**Pattern drill (7)** This is used for marking things such as darts, pockets and any other marking points within the pattern piece. The pattern drill will punch a hole of $1/16$–$3/16$ in (2–4 mm) into the pattern. The position of the punch hole can then be marked with chalk or thread on to the fabric.

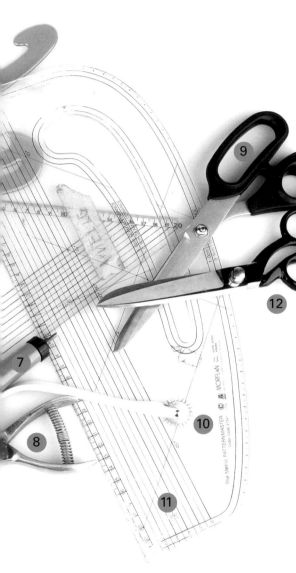

**Pattern notcher (8)** This is used for marking the edge of the pattern pieces by taking out a small square for each balance point. This should only be used on pattern paper, thin sheets of plastic or card—not on fabric.

**Paper scissors (9)** These are—as their name suggests—only used for paper, in order to keep the blades sharp.

**Tracing wheel (10)** This is used to trace a line from one piece of paper or pattern on to another directly underneath it.

**Pattern master (11)** This is used to create lines and curves and to check angles.

**Fabric Scissors/Shears (12)** These scissors or shears are to be used when cutting fabric, again in order to keep the blades sharp.

**Small Scissors/Snips (13)** These are helpful when cutting threads whilst stitching and also can be used to help unpick mistakes. Especially good for very fine and intricate work.

**Pencils** (not shown) Your pencil can be a mechanical or traditional pencil, but should be no softer than HB. This is to ensure sharp and accurate lines.

**Aluminium meter ruler** (not shown) This is essential for drawing and connecting longer, straight lines.

# Silhouettes

First impressions of an outfit are created by its silhouette—the overall shape created by a garment. Before qualities such as the detail, fabric or texture of the garment can be considered, the silhouette of the garment is an important initial decision in the design and construction process.

## The importance of silhouette

Silhouette is fundamental to the preliminary stages of the design process in order to determine which parts of the body will be emphasized and why. Once these decisions are made, it is up to the pattern cutter and designer to start contemplating how the design can be physically constructed and, if necessary, supported and structured using underpinnings and foundations. Many materials and techniques can be used to shape a silhouette (see chapter seven: Support and structure). For example, using shoulder pads to widen the shoulder can create an illusion of a small waist and narrow hips.

## Proportion and bodylines

Proportion refers to the comparative relations and dimensions of the various parts of a whole outfit. A combination of garments can look messy or can work in harmony. For example, the ways in which a jacket, a skirt and a pair of boots relate to one another will add to the sense of proportion and balance conveyed by the outfit as a whole.

Proportions can be changed fairly easily using various construction methods. For example, moving a hemline, waistline, pocket, seam or dart position can dramatically alter the balance of width and length on an individual body shape. Choice of fabric texture and color can also add to the overall effect conveyed by the cut and shape of a garment.

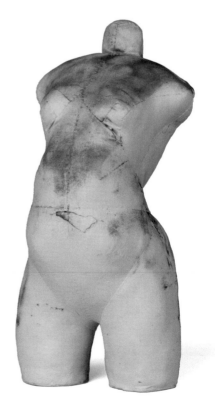

**1.2 Sculptured ceramic mannequin by Helen Manley.**

## The change of silhouette over time

Throughout history, fashion has always
reflected the wealth of the nation,
the status of individuals and cultural
representation over time. See p. 142 for
a more detailed look at the history of
supported and structured garments.

1800    1830    1895    1900

1911    1912    1920

**1.3 The changing shape and proportions of fashion
in the Western world over the course of history.**

New Look, 1947

# Sizing and grading

Designs for a garment can be cut and made to fit an individual customer, or they can be graded and altered to fit wearers of differing sizes. Either way, a full and detailed knowledge of sizing and grading is essential for any designer hoping to create a beautifully fitting garment. Being able to translate body proportions to paper and back to a three-dimensional garment takes much practice, and careful attention to detail is important.

**1.4 A flexible tape measure is essential for the sizing and grading process.**

## Sizing

Womenswear sizing is based on measurements of height, bust, waist and hips. In the UK, sizing starts at size 6 and goes up to size 22 (the best-selling sizes are 10, 12 and 14). European sizes start at size 34 (which is equivalent to size 6) and go up to size 52. American equivalents range from a size 2 to 18. However, as the fashion industry becomes increasingly sophisticated and complex, it is becoming much easier to find other size ranges to accompany these, such as petite, tall or half-size.

Menswear sizing is universally made up of a chest measurement for a jacket and a waist and inside leg measurement for trousers. Shirt sizes are given by the neck measurement.

In childrenswear, the principal variable is usually height so sizing is governed mainly by age.

Measurements for each size can be taken from charts in pattern cutting books but, where possible, it is always best to take real measurements from live models.

## Grading

Grading is the process of scaling a pattern to a different size by incrementing important points of the pattern according to a set of given measurements, such as the British Standard sizing chart. Grading is a very specialized area in pattern cutting that not many professionals master. The secret is to know where the pattern needs changing to fit the decrease and increase in body size. Such increments can vary from 1 ¾₁₆ to 2 in (3 to 5 cm), depending on the garment range.

Many manufacturers use the British Standard sizing chart, which was first established in the 1950s and has changed over the years to accommodate changes in lifestyle. The United States has its own sizing chart, and many other nations have worked out standard sizing for their own needs. Factors such as culture and diet have great influence on a country's average body shape. For example, northern European body shapes are generally tall and large, whereas the average body shape in the Far East is shorter in height and slimmer in stature. For these reasons, a design house must always carefully consider the market it wants to sell to.

When grading a pattern, make sure that all corresponding seams, notches and punch marks match before starting the grading process. Grading can be done by hand with a metric grader's set square, pattern master or an L-square ruler, as well as by computer using a specific program, such as Lectra or Gerber.

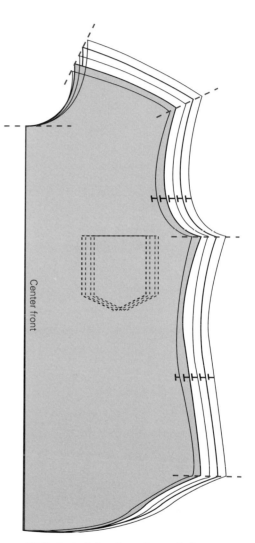

Center front

**1.5 Technical drawing of a graded pattern piece.**

## Taking measurements

**Neck girth (1)** This is the measurement around the base of the neckline.

**Shoulder length (2)** This is measured from the neckline to end of shoulder bone.

**Top bust girth (3)** This is measured around the body, under the arm but above the bust in a horizontal line.

**Bust girth (4)** This is measured around the fullest point of the bust in a horizontal line.

**Under bust girth (5)** This is measured around the rib cage under the bust in a horizontal line.

**Waist girth (6)** This is the measurement around the narrowest part of the waist (natural waistline) in a horizontal line.

**High hip girth (7)** This is measured around the abdomen about 3–4 in (8–10 cm) below the waistline in a horizontal line.

**Hip girth (8)** This is the measurement around the fullest part of the hip in a horizontal line.

**Arm length (9)** This is measured from shoulder point, past the elbow, down to the wrist with the arm slightly bent.

**Front length (10)** This is measured from the shoulder/neckline cross point, past the nipple and down to the natural waistline.

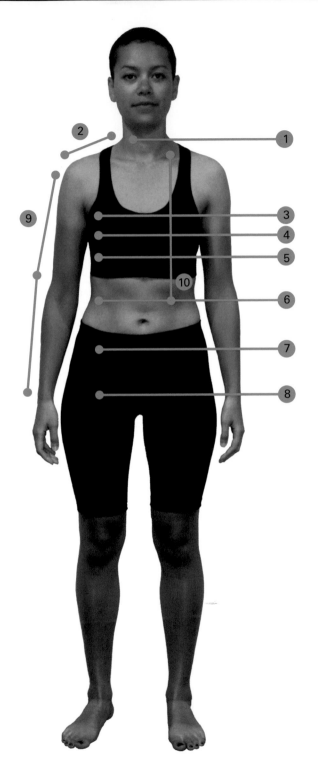

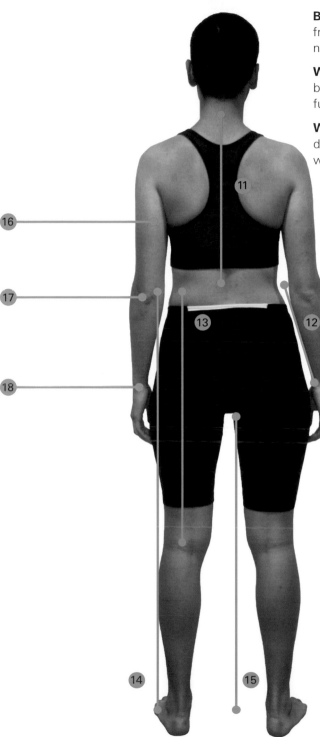

**Back length (11)** This is measured from the nape of the neck to the natural waistline.

**Waist to hip (12)** This is the distance between the natural waistline and the fullest point of the hipline.

**Waist to knee (13)** This is the distance between the natural waistline and the knee.

**Outside leg (14)** This is the distance from the natural waistline to the floor or outside ankle.

**Inside leg (15)** This is the distance from the inside crotch to the floor or inside ankle.

**Bicep (16)** This is the measurement around the top of the arm.

**Elbow (17)** This is measured around the width of the elbow.

**Wrist girth (18)** This is measured around the width of the wrist.

## Taking measurements

When taking measurements, make sure that the tape is neither too loose nor too tight around the body.

There are many more measurements that can be taken. If you are constructing a shirt with a tight fitted sleeve, for example, the measurements of the bicep (16), elbow (17) and wrist (18) also need to be taken into consideration. This is to avoid the fit being too tight or too loose on the arms.

# Blocks and patterns

Blocks and patterns enable the designer to render something flat (paper or fabric) into something three-dimensional. They are laid on to fabric, cut out and assembled together using seams. In order to create well-made garments, it is essential that the designer fully understands the techniques used in order to make pattern cutting as straightforward and accurate as possible.

## The block

A block (also known as a sloper) is a two-dimensional template for a basic garment form (for example, a bodice shape or fitted skirt) that can be modified into a more elaborate design. Blocks are constructed using measurements taken from a size chart or a live model and do not show any style lines or seam allowance.

Blocks must, however, include basic amounts of allowance for ease and comfort; for instance, a tight-fitting bodice block would not have as much allowance added into the construction as a block for an outerwear garment might. A fitted bodice block would also have darts added into the draft to shape the garment to the waist and bust, whereas a block for a loose-fitting overcoat would not need these.

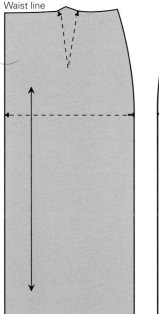

**1.6 A sample skirt block.**

## The pattern

A pattern is developed from a design sketch using a block. The designer or pattern cutter will add to the block by introducing style lines, drapes, pleats, pockets and other adjustments to create an original pattern.

The final pattern features a series of different shaped pieces of paper that are traced on to fabric and then cut out, before being seamed together to create a three-dimensional garment. Each pattern piece contains "notches" or points that correspond to a point on the adjoining pattern piece, enabling whoever is making the garment to join the seams together accurately. The pieces need to fit together precisely; otherwise the garment will not look right when sewn together, and it will not fit well on the body.

When the block modification is finished, seam allowance is added to the pattern. To perfect a pattern, a toile (a garment made out of a cheap fabric such as calico) is made and fitted on to a live fitting model. Adjustments can be made on the toile before being transferred to the pattern.

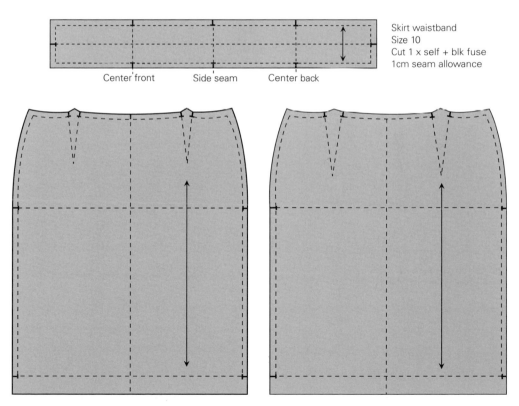

Skirt waistband
Size 10
Cut 1 x self + blk fuse
1cm seam allowance

Center front    Side seam    Center back

**1.7 The translation to pattern.**

## Samples

A sample is the first version of a garment made in real fabric. It is this garment that goes on the catwalk or into a press/showroom. Samples are produced for womenswear in sizes 8–10 (6–8 US) to fit the models. Once the sale book is closed, the samples are stored in the company's archive. Some samples of past collections are taken out by designers for photo shoots, events such as premieres and for reference or possible inspiration for future collections.

Bust

Waist

Hip

**1.8 The block and its corresponding measurements.**

## How the measurements relate to the block

Whether taking individual measurements or using a size chart, the main measurements (bust girth, waist girth, waist-to-hip length and hip girth) will give a good indication of the body shape the design is intended to fit.

Secondary measurements may also be taken from an individual or from a size

chart. This may be the length of skirt, for example, when drafting a skirt block.

Darts can be used to control excess fabric and to create shape on a garment when stitched together. Curves are added to create shape depending on the nature and purpose of the block.

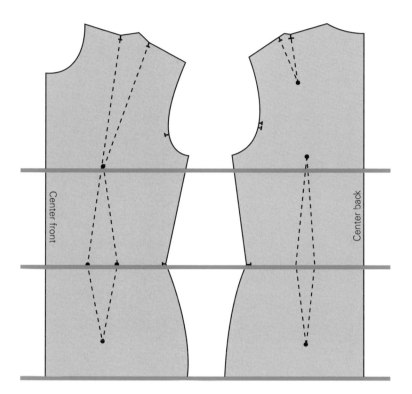

Center front

Center back

## How to start a set of blocks

A set of blocks can be cut for one individual in order to create bespoke/couture garments. Design houses will often create their own set of blocks to complement their special ethos and design philosophy. When starting a set of blocks, it may help to ask the following questions:

What is my target group: women, children or men?

What will be the smallest and the largest size in my size chart?

What is my sample size?

What is my collection range: lingerie, tailoring, streetwear?

The answers to these questions will make it much easier to cut the right blocks from which to create original patterns for each collection.

## Inspired practitioners
### Martine Rose, Menswear Designer

Martine is an acclaimed London-based menswear designer and consultant. She sells internationally to stores such as Machine A, Barney's, Opening Ceremony, Broken Arm, Gr8 and Joyrich. Martine has gained the prestigious British Fashion Council sponsored NEWGEN award and consults on an international platform, as well as designing for her eponymous menswear label.

**What is your approach to design?**
I start with a sense of what I would like to develop, a mood, a feeling and then I start to research around this collecting imagery to bring the story together. There tends to be an over-all subject, but sometimes the imagery can reflect more about color or mood than actual pieces. In addition to this, I also source vintage pieces around this theme that I will use as a foundation to build upon. From that point, I start with an overall silhouette that I would like to work upon, and start work in more detail on the pieces themselves.

**How important is the construction process in the way you work?**
Construction is very important, as I tend to explore proportion and volume a lot. The construction allows me to exaggerate these whilst still being functional and wearable.

**Where do you begin with material research?**
The direction is largely dictated to by the research, season and the pieces I source. Then it often starts with suppliers I know that have the fabric that I am looking for or similar—often it will throw up some surprises.

**Being a menswear designer, how do you balance detail with innovation of shape?**
That's the toughest part—traditional menswear is really focused on the detail, small changes to pockets, cut etc. However, my approach is far more rooted in the sense of proportion and this will often involve the detail. It is extremely important, however, in menswear that the garment is completely functional and works with the same convenience and ease that a traditional piece would.

**Any advice for any aspiring designers?**
Go for it, follow your instincts, trust them, be brave and get a good accountant.

## Task

### Getting started: blocks, measurements, machinery

1. Get a feel for your tools and practice how to use them. Try the following:
   - Draw straight continuous lines with your pattern master or set square.
   - Add ⅜ in (1 cm), ¼ in (0.7 cm) and ³⁄₁₆ in (0.5 cm) seam allowance to these lines.
   - Draw curves and circles using your pattern master and French curves.
   - Trace some of these shapes out onto fresh pattern paper and use the marks to draw new lines.
2. Consider who your target audience is and create a set of blocks. Take your measurements from a live model. Create the following with no seam allowance (also known as NSA):
   - A close fitting block
   - An overgarment block
   - A trouser block

   Once checked and corrected, transfer these blocks to cards and keep as templates for following exercises and for future use.

3. Familiarize yourself with an industrial or domestic sewing machine. Ensure you have the correct bobbin and machine feet for your machine. Practice the following:
   - Sewing in straight lines
   - Sewing in curves and circles
   - Changing stitch length and also test tension

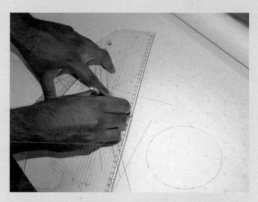

**1.9 Practicing drawing lines with a pattern master.**

**1.10 Taking measurements of the body.**

**1.11 Threading up an industrial sewing machine.**

# Pattern Cutting

Like all craft skills, pattern cutting can at first seem difficult and intimidating. But with a basic understanding of the rules to be followed (and broken!), the aspiring designer will soon learn interesting, challenging and creative approaches to pattern cutting. To draw the right style line in the correct position on a garment takes experience and practice. Designers who have been cutting patterns for twenty years can still learn something new—the process of learning never stops. This makes creative pattern cutting a fascinating process.

In this chapter, we introduce the meaning of a drafted block and how to turn it into a pattern from a design drawing. We take a look at dart manipulation as well as pocket, collar and sleeve construction. You will be introduced to cutting techniques and bias-cut garments. You will also learn about the fitting process: how to fit the toile and alter the pattern accordingly. Finally, we take a look at the different ways of laying and cutting patterns from fabric.

2.1 Chalayan SS16.

# How to read a design drawing

This is the point at which pattern cutting becomes much more creative and exciting. Once the design has been completed, the process of breathing life into a flat design drawing in order to achieve an actual garment can begin. To be able to achieve a beautiful garment shape takes time and experience. Remember, nothing ever happens without practicing your skills—don't be disheartened if it doesn't work first time round. All outstanding fashion designers and creative pattern cutters have worked for years to perfect their skills.

## Translating drawing to block

The translation of a design drawing to pattern requires an eye trained for proportions. Most design drawings are sketched on a figure with distorted proportions. The legs and neck are too long and the figure too slender. These sketches are often inspiring and wonderful to look at but unfortunately give a false image of the human body and it is a key task of the pattern cutter to address this. Drawing a technical or flat drawing of the garment can also help understand the proportion of the design.

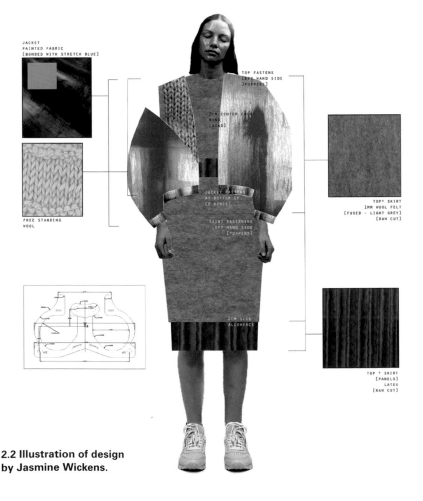

**2.2 Illustration of design by Jasmine Wickens.**

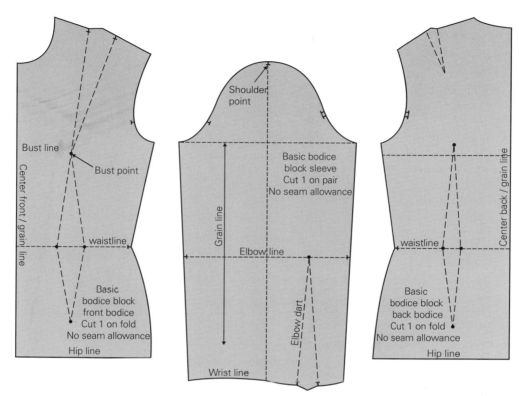

Bust line

Center front / grain line

Bust point

waistline

Basic
bodice block
front bodice
Cut 1 on fold
No seam allowance

Hip line

Shoulder
point

Grain line

Basic bodice
block sleeve
Cut 1 on pair
No seam allowance

Elbow line

Elbow dart

Wrist line

waistline

Center back / grain line

Basic
bodice block
back bodice
Cut 1 on fold
No seam allowance

Hip line

**2.3 A basic bodice block.**

## How to mark the block

It is essential when cutting a block or a pattern that the correct information is supplied. A bodice block, for example, has to show the horizontal lines of the bust-, waist- and hiplines. Parts of the block such as the waist and bust points should be notched or punch marked (holes and notches indicate where the separate pieces of fabric will be attached to one another) and the grain line must be indicated. This will clearly show the position in which the pattern should be placed on the fabric. Additional information must be written clearly in the center of the block, including whether it is a front or back piece, a tight- or loose-fitted bodice block and if it is the sample size, preferably with the measurements and any allowances to be made when constructing the block.

Once the pattern has been constructed, the seam allowance can be added. Seam allowance can vary in size from a narrow ³⁄₁₆ in (0.5 cm) for a neckline (to avoid having to clip or trim the seam) to 1 in (2.5 cm) in the center back of trousers (to be able to let some out if the waist gets too tight). Seams that are to be joined together should always be the same width. Mark the width of the seam allowance on the pattern.

Usually, the block ends up being divided into further pattern pieces. At this point, therefore, the information should be reconsidered accordingly, except the grain line and front or back information, which are always transferred to the new pieces.

## Marking symbols on a pattern

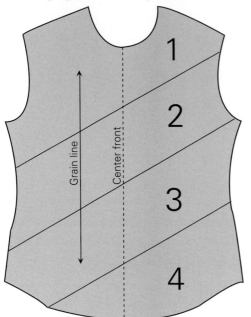

**2.4 Number sections before cutting a pattern apart to avoid confusion.**

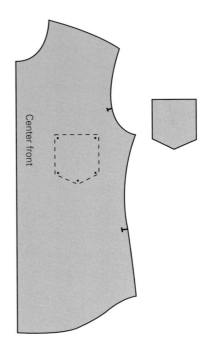

**2.5 Position marks, such as for pockets, are hole-punched into the pattern.**

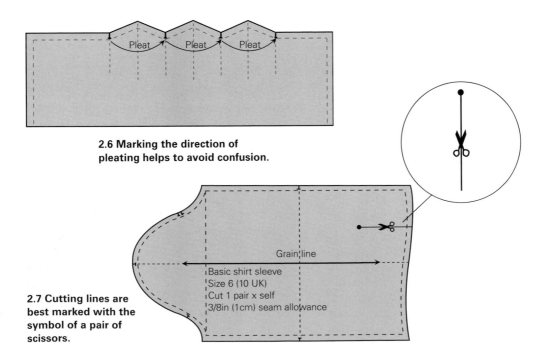

**2.6 Marking the direction of pleating helps to avoid confusion.**

**2.7 Cutting lines are best marked with the symbol of a pair of scissors.**

Grain line

Basic shirt sleeve
Size 6 (10 UK)
Cut 1 pair x self
3/8in (1cm) seam allowance

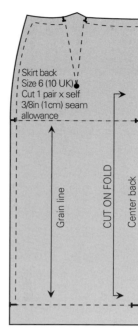
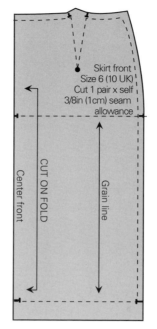

Skirt front
Size 6 (10 UK)
Cut 1 pair x self
3/8in (1cm) seam
allowance

Skirt back
Size 6 (10 UK)
Cut 1 pair x self
3/8in (1cm) seam
allowance

Center front

CUT ON FOLD

Grain line

Grain line

CUT ON FOLD

Center back

**2.8 If the piece is to be cut on the fabric fold (so it does not have a seam), indicate this with the message "cut on fold," otherwise create the full mirrored piece.**

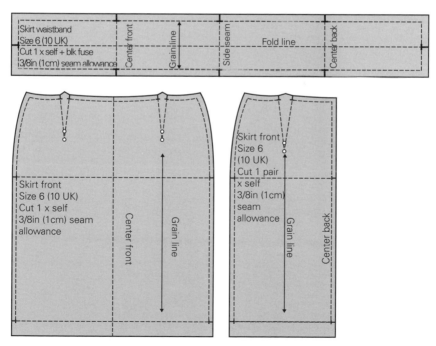

Skirt waistband
Size 6 (10 UK)
Cut 1 x self + blk fuse
3/8in (1cm) seam allowance

Center front

Grainline

Side seam

Fold line

Center back

Skirt front
Size 6 (10 UK)
Cut 1 x self
3/8in (1cm) seam
allowance

Center front

Grain line

Skirt front
Size 6
(10 UK)
Cut 1 pair
x self
3/8in (1cm)
seam
allowance

Grain line

Center back

**2.9 Cut 1 x self (or cut 1 x) = cut the one piece only.**
**Cut 1 pair x self (or cut 2 x) = cut two pieces.**
**C.F. = center front.**
**C.B. = center back.**

# Dart manipulation

Darts control excess fabric to create shape on a garment. They can be stitched together end to end or to a zero point, also known as the pivotal point (such as the bust point). Dart manipulation is the most creative and flexible part of pattern cutting. The possibilities are endless, and the designer's imagination is the only limitation. Darts can be turned into pleats, gathers or style lines. Their positioning on the body is very important; not only do these techniques create fit, shape and volume, they also change the style and design of the garment.

## Example of dart manipulation on a bodice block

Design analysis: asymmetrical design with intersecting darts coming from the waist and ending at the bust point.

1. Trace bodice block on fold. When copying the left side of the front block, transfer the complete waist and bust dart into the armhole. Then copy the right side of the front block on to the left front block (center front attached to center front), and transfer the complete waist and bust dart into the armhole.

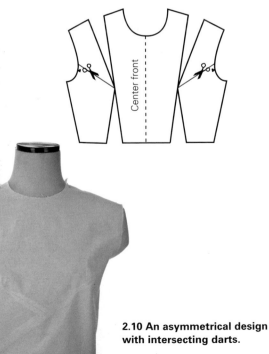

2. Draw in the slashing lines according to your design.

3. Cut along the slash lines, up to the bust point (pivotal point). Close up the darts and tape them down.

4. Add seam allowances and mark the dart ends with a hole-punch as well as notching the position of the left dart, center front and seam allowances. Mark the grain line (in this case the center front) and add information such as "front, right-side-up, cut x 1."
5. If required, the armholes and neckline can be altered for more comfort. A back pattern can be cut to fit the front design.
6. The pattern is now ready to be cut out of calico and made into a toile for a fitting.

**2.10 An asymmetrical design with intersecting darts.**

**2.11 Daks AW15.**

# Slash and spread

This method is used to add extra volume and flare. The technique involves creating slash lines that reach from one end of the pattern to the other, sometimes ending on a pivotal point like a dart ending. These slash lines will then be opened up for added volume and flare.

## Using slash and spread techniques

Slash and spread techniques can be used to convert a straight skirt pattern into a skirt with flare. The most basic way of doing this is to divide the pattern up into equal pieces from hem to waist, and open them up by equal amounts all the way round. Redraw the hemline as a smooth curve.

To create asymmetric flare, as shown in 2.13 and 2.14, the pattern is divided into two and slash lines are marked on to one of these halves. These are cut along from hem to waist and opened up (spread) with equal amounts added into each "slash." This creates flare on one side of the skirt. Pleats have also been added to the waistline. Drawing in an angular hemline creates the asymmetric point.

> ### Tips when using slash-and-spread method
>
> When using the slash and spread method, remember that the position you slash in is the exact position the fabric will flare out. So when slashing into one side only, the flare will not spread across but only appear on one side.

**2.12 Skirt constructed by slash and spread method to gain flare.**

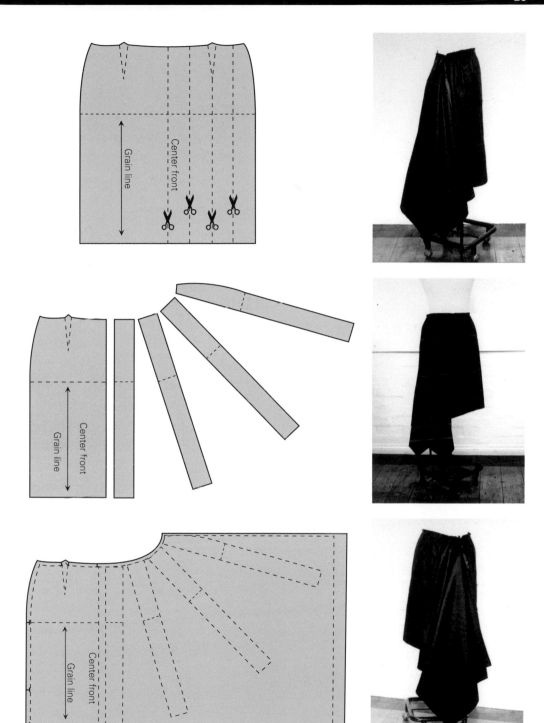

**2.13–2.14 Asymmetric skirt that has been opened up on one side only.**

# Sleeves

Sleeve construction is a very special part of pattern cutting. Sleeves can be part of the bodice (laid-on sleeve) or set into an armhole (set-in sleeve). Without any other design features added, a garment can look outstanding by simply creating an interesting sleeve design. The most basic sleeve block is the one-piece (set-in) sleeve, which can be varied as shown in 2.17a–f. Different sleeve blocks can be developed from the one-piece block, such as the two-piece sleeve and laid-on sleeves, including raglan, kimono/batwing and dolman designs.

**2.15 Balmain AW15.**

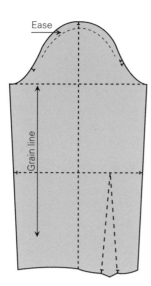

**2.16 A sleeve block for a set-in sleeve, showing the part where the sleeve can be eased into the armhole.**

## Constructing sleeves

When constructing a set-in sleeve, the measurement of the armhole is essential. Therefore, the bodice front and back are constructed first and once the measurement of the armhole is established, ease is added according to the type of block (jacket block, fitted bodice block and so on). Ease is added to a pattern to allow for extra comfort or movement. As well as allowing the sleeve to sit comfortably in the armhole, ease will also affect the fit and silhouette of a garment. Ease is distributed between the front notch and the double back notch of the sleeve (see 2.16). In some set-in sleeve designs, the ease is taken across the shoulder to achieve a round appearance over the shoulder point. A sleeve is sitting comfortably in the armhole when it aligns exactly with, or is set slightly in front of, the side seam of the bodice.

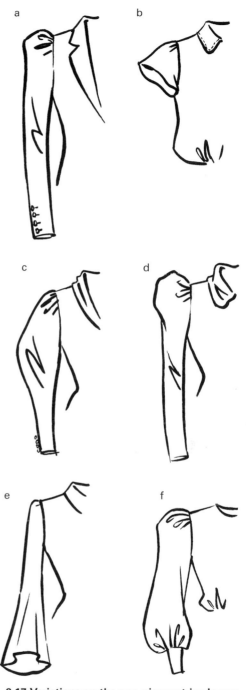

**2.17 Variations on the one-piece set-in sleeve:**

**a. peak sleeve**      **d. Juliet sleeve**
**b. cap sleeve**       **e. trumpet sleeve**
**c. leg o' mutton sleeve**   **f. bishop sleeve**

## One-piece and two-piece sleeves

There are differences between one-piece and two-piece sleeves, the major one being the amount of seams that are used. A one-piece sleeve has only one seam placed under the arm at the side seam position. Therefore, the seam cannot be seen when the arm is relaxed. The two-piece sleeve has two seams: One is placed at the back, running from the position of the back double notch down to the wrist, past the elbow. The second seam is moved a little to the front, from under the arm side seam position (still not visible from the front). The look of a two-piece sleeve is more shapely, and it has a slight bend to the front. As such, it is possible to get a closer fit with a two-piece sleeve because of its extra seam. One-piece sleeves are used for a more casual look, whereas two-piece sleeves are mostly seen on garments such as tailored jackets or coats.

## Laid-on sleeve

The laid-on sleeve is part of the bodice. Once constructed, either a part of the armhole remains or there is no armhole at all.

A laid-on sleeve is most commonly constructed by separating the one-piece sleeve through the shoulder notch straight down to the wristline to gain a front piece and a back piece (see 2.18). The next step is to align the front piece of the sleeve with the bodice's front shoulder, and the back sleeve with the bodice's back shoulder. From this point onwards several styles can be developed, such as batwing or kimono, raglan, gusset and dolman sleeves. The sleeve can be laid on at variant angles—the greater the angle, the more excess fabric and, therefore, a greater range of arm movement.

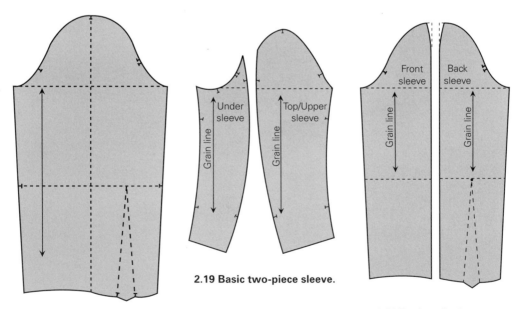

2.19 Basic two-piece sleeve.

2.20 Basic split sleeve.

2.18 Basic one-piece sleeve.

## Gusset sleeve

To extend the lift (a technical term for moveability of the arm) in a sleeve, a gusset can be added. A gusset is traditionally a diamond-shaped piece, which is inserted into a slit in the underarm section of the sleeve.

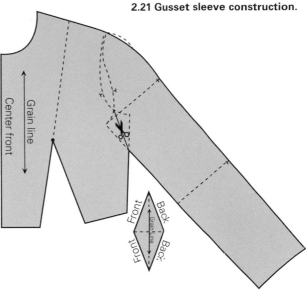

**2.21 Gusset sleeve construction.**

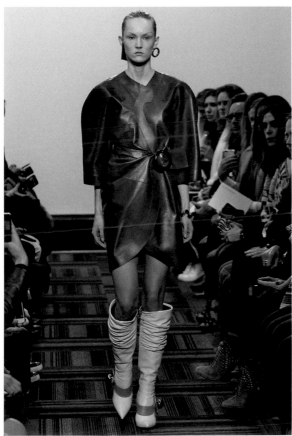

**2.22 5 J.W.Anderson AW15.**

## Kimono sleeve

Like a Japanese sleeve, the
kimono sleeve is cut in one
with the bodice. The seams
can run from the outer- or
underarm.

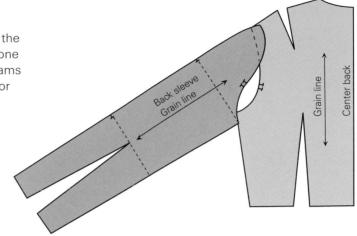

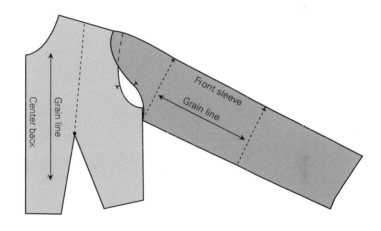

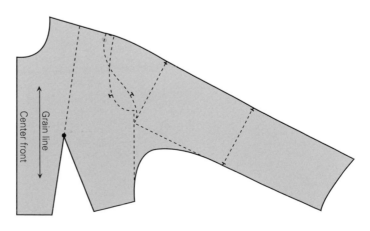

**2.23 Acne Studios AW15.**

**2.24–2.26 Preparation for a kimono sleeve construction.**

## Raglan sleeve

The raglan sleeve has a dropped shoulder design. It is constructed to have a seam running from the neckline on a slant into the underarm on front and back.

### Lord Raglan

Lord Raglan was a commander of the British troops during the Crimean War. His right arm was injured at the Battle of Waterloo and had to be amputated. As a result, he got himself a coat designed with a special sleeve—the raglan sleeve.

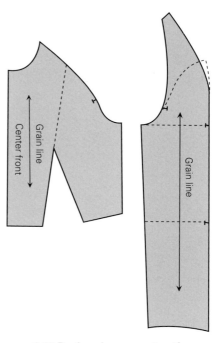

**2.28 Raglan sleeve construction.**

**2.27 Trench coat with raglan sleeve.**

## Dolman sleeve

Originally named after the 1870s coat/wrap that looks like a cape from the back with lowered armholes and set-in sleeves in the front. The dolman sleeve today has lots of fabric under the arms and can be fitted to the wrist, still looking like a cape from the back. The sleeve construction is illustrated in 2.30–2.32. The original back bodice construction (2.30) shows the laid-on sleeve. The final pattern pieces show the front bodice that has been extended underarm (2.31) and the back bodice with the laid-on sleeve (2.32).

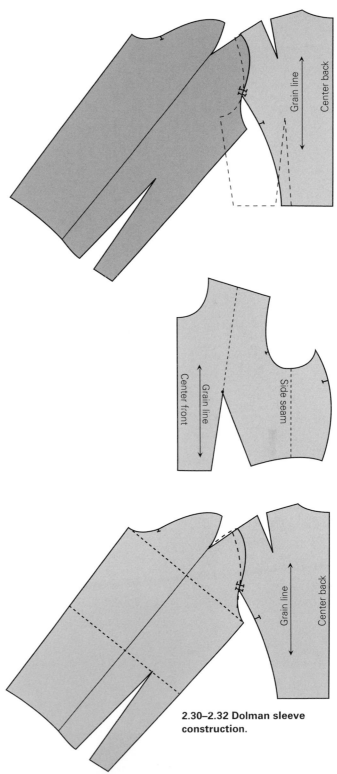

**2.29 Example of a dolman sleeve.**

**2.30–2.32 Dolman sleeve construction.**

## Pleated, darted and gathered

The one-piece sleeve block can be adapted in countless ways. These patterns illustrate how the sleeve block can be altered to create puffed, pleated and darted sleeves.

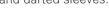

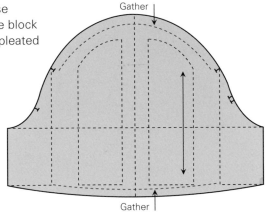

Gather

Gather

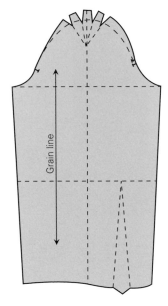

Grain line

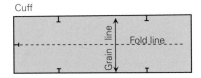

Cuff

Grain line

Fold line

**2.34 Pattern for a puff sleeve construction with gathers on the sleeve head and small cuff.**

**2.33 Pattern construction of a darted sleeve head.**

**2.35 Vintage dress with pleated sleeve head.**

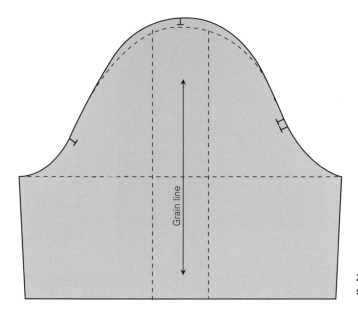

**2.36 Preparations for a pleated sleeve head construction.**

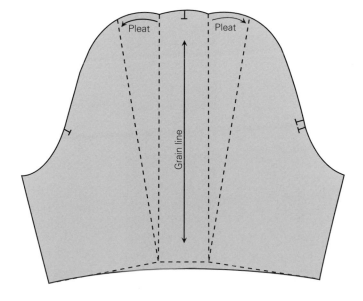

**2.37 Pattern construction of a pleated sleeve head.**

# Collars

The collar is a versatile design feature that will enhance the style of a garment. It is attached to the neckline of the garment and allows the size and shape of the neckline to vary. Collars come in all shapes and sizes and the most common are the stand-up/mandarin, shirt, flat, sailor and lapel collar constructions.

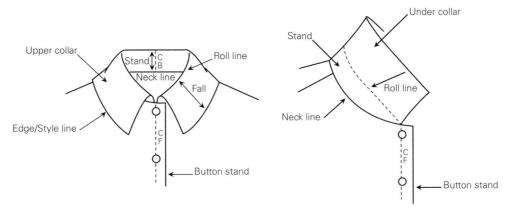

**2.38 Technical drawing showing the key elements of a basic collar construction.**

## Drafting variations

Collars can be constructed in three basic ways. The first method is a right-angle construction, used for stand-up collars, shirt collars and small flat collars such as Peter Pan and Eton collars.

Secondly, they can be constructed by joining the shoulders of the front and back bodice together to construct the collar directly on top of the bodice block. This technique is used to construct sailor collars and bigger versions of flat collars. The advantage of using this method is that the correct outer length of the collar construction results automatically, however large the collar or neckline extension is.

Third, the lapel construction, is extended from the center front, from the breaking point (usually where the first button or fastening is) toward the shoulder. By extending the break/roll line, a collar construction can be added. A version of this is the shawl collar, where the collar extends from the fabric of the garment on to the lapel without being sewn on.

## Basic collar measurements

The measurement of the neckline on the pattern has to be taken in order to construct a collar. Therefore, if the neckline is to be changed according to the design, do this before cutting the collar pattern.

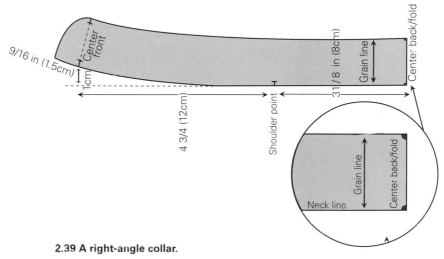

**2.39 A right-angle collar.**

**2.40 Flat collar on a pea coat.**

## Right-angle construction collars

Right-angle collars are constructed by drawing the center back line and the neckline at a right angle to each other and adding all measurements. Variations of this basic construction include mandarin or stand-up collars and shirt collars, which can have either integrated or separate stands.

If the center front of the collar is constructed higher than the neckline and the center back point, the collar will sit close to the neck. If the center back of the collar is constructed higher than the neckline and the center front point, the collar will sit away from the neck.

Example: ½ neck size = 20cm (Back neck length = 8cm/Front neck length = 12cm) Button stand allowance 1.5cm

Basic stand-up collar

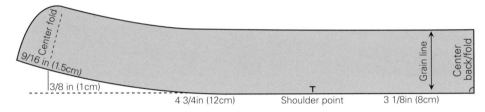

Tighter fitting stand-up collar

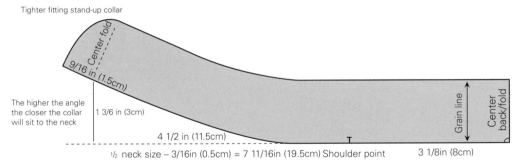

**2.41 Stand-up collar. The shorter the top edge of the collar, the closer the fit.**

**2.42 Menswear shirt with stand-up collar.**

## Flat collars

A flat collar, with or without a stand construction included, traditionally meets in the center front without an over- and under-wrap (the over- and under-wrap is an extension from the center front to create space for the button and buttonhole). The collar has a small stand height (generally between ¾₁₆ in (0.5 cm) and ⁹₁₆ in (1.5 cm) and lies comfortably along the shoulder.

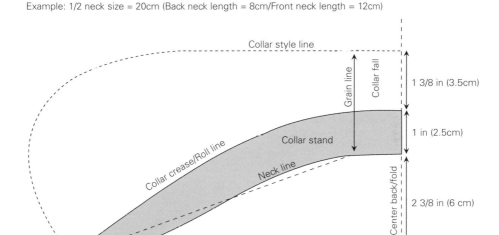

Example: 1/2 neck size = 20cm (Back neck length = 8cm/Front neck length = 12cm)

**2.43 Peter Pan collar pattern.**

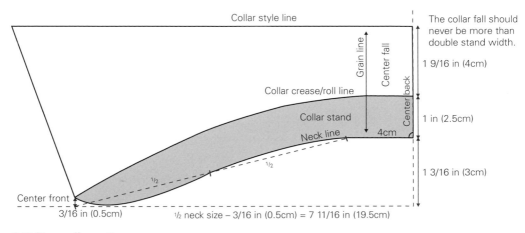

Example: 1/2 neck size = 7 7/8 in (20cm) (back neck length = 3 1/8 in (8cm)/front neck length = 4 3/4 in (12cm))

The collar fall should never be more than double stand width.

**2.44 Eton collar pattern.**

Example:1/2 neck size = 7 7/8 in (20cm)
(Back neck length = 3 1/9 in (8cm)/Front neck length = 14 3/4 in (12cm)) Button stand allowance 9/16 in (1.5cm)

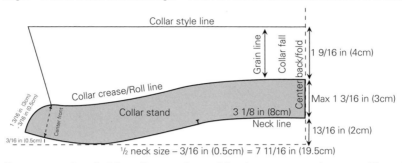

Collar style line

Grain line

Collar fall

Center back/fold

1 9/16 in (4cm)

Collar crease/Roll line

Collar stand

3 1/8 in (8cm)

Max 1 3/16 in (3cm)

Neck line

13/16 in (2cm)

Center front

1 3/16 in (3cm)– 3/16 in (0.5cm)

3/16 in (0.5cm)

½ neck size – 3/16 in (0.5cm) = 7 11/16 in (19.5cm)

**2.45 Shirt collar construction.** A shirt collar stand can either be separate or integrated into the collar construction. Integrated stands are used for smaller shirt collars for childrenswear.

Example:1/2 neck size = 7 7/8 in (20cm) (back neck length = 3 1/9 in (8cm)/
front neck length = 4 3/4 in (12cm)). Button stand allowance 9/16 in (1.5cm)

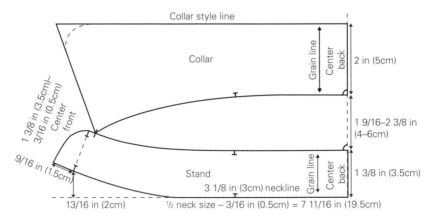

Collar style line

Grain line

Center back

2 in (5cm)

Collar

1 9/16–2 3/8 in (4–6cm)

Stand

Grain line

Center back

1 3/8 in (3.5cm)

3 1/8 in (3cm) neckline

1 3/8 in (3.5cm)– 3/16 in (0.5cm)

Center front

9/16 in (1.5cm)

13/16 in (2cm)

½ neck size – 3/16 in (0.5cm) = 7 11/16 in (19.5cm)

**2.46 Shirt collar with separate stand construction.** A shirt collar with a separate stand is closer to the neck than a collar with an integrated stand. A separate stand allows the designer to build more height into the construction, creating a more severe and military looking collar.

## Button-down collar

The button-down collar is a variation of the shirt collar. Its design was inspired in England at a polo match where the players had their collars attached to keep them from flapping in the wind. The "button-down" can be worn informally with the collar open as well as dressed up with a tie or bow-tie.

**2.48 Martine Rose SS13.**

**2.47 A shirt collar with separate stand.**

## Collars joined at the shoulder

This shape of collar was originally copied from the naval uniform. The look is traditionally a V-shaped neckline in the front and a long square panel that lies flat down the back. The sailor collar construction is used not only to cut the sailor style but also for other big collar shapes.

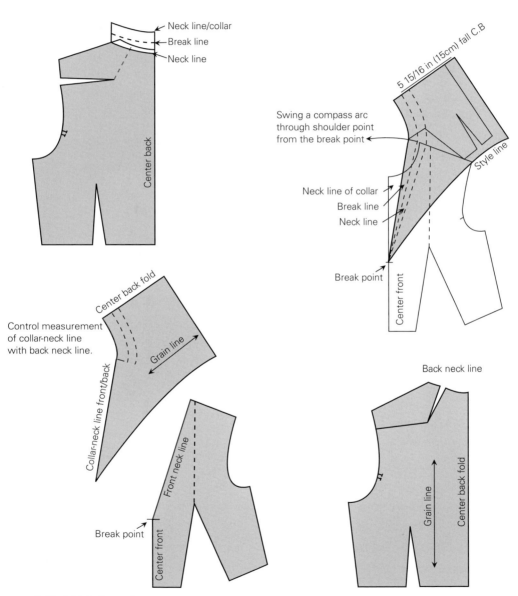

2.49–2.52 Sailor collar construction.

2.53 Celine SS07.

## Tailored collars

A lapel collar is a V-shape neckline with the lapel grown on. The extension (the lapel) is folded back and reveals the facing. It is the front section of a jacket, coat, blouse or shirt. The lapel is usually joined to a collar and both can be cut in various shapes. A variation of a lapel is a shawl collar, a construction whereby the lapel and collar are joined together. The breaking point is dependant on style and can define a tailored jacket. The break point is usually where the first button or fastening sits.

Before a lapel can be constructed, the designer must establish the position of the breaking point and also whether the garment is to have a single- or double-breasted style.

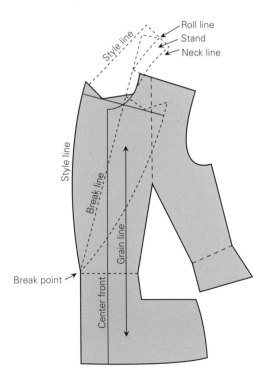

**2.54–2.55 Double-breasted lapel collar construction.**

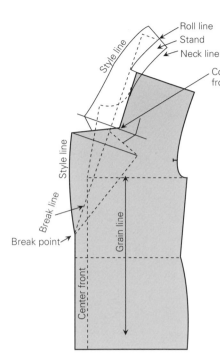

**2.56–2.57 Single-breasted lapel collar construction.**

## Top- and-under-collars

A tailored collar can be constructed in two parts: the lapel and collar. The collar has a top layer (the top-collar) and an underside layer (the under-collar). The top-collar should be bigger in size with added millimeters around the edges of the under-collar ( ⅛ in [2–3 mm] on a fine to middleweight fabric and ³⁄₁₆ in [4–5 mm] on a thicker fabric). The top-collar is made bigger to prevent the under-collar from showing beyond the stitching line.

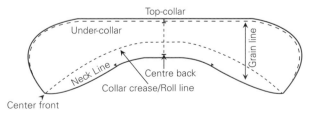

**2.58 Top- and under-collar construction.**

# Pockets

Before the fifteenth century, pockets were simply pouches worn attached to a belt. It was not until the mid-eighteenth century that dressmakers started to introduce small pockets into the waistline seams of dresses. These days, pockets are not only traditional and functional, they can also be used to define the style of a garment. Pockets fall into two basic categories: patch pockets, where the pocket bag sits on the outside of the garment; and set-in pockets, where the pocket bag is set inside the garment. The set-in pocket opening may be hidden or made into a design feature.

## Designing pockets

Pockets should be functional, so try to create pockets that are large enough to put a hand in. Remember that men's hands are larger than women's.

Some tailors add a pleat in the center of the inside pocket bag to allow for shaped objects, such as keys, to go inside the pocket bag without pulling and showing a stretch mark on the jacket outside.

The position of the pocket on the garment is very important. Not only is it a focal point, it also needs to be easily accessed. The best way to find the pocket position is to fit the garment on a life model and ask him or her to point out a comfortable position for the pocket mouth.

When grading a garment with pockets, make sure to grade the pocket within natural proportions.

When using slant, continental or side seam pockets in trousers, make sure to continue the pocket bag into the center front zip fly. This method will keep the pocket bags in place and create a nice finish in the inside of the garment.

When constructing welt or jetted pockets in the back of trousers or skirts, sew the pocket bag into the waistband for stability.

The pocket mouth (this is the part where the pocket is worked in) should always be secured through an interlining.

Inside pockets sometimes have buttons to enable the pocket bag to be closed. Cover the button up with a triangular piece of lining to avoid the button leaving marks on garments worn under the jacket. It also prevents the button from being caught in the garment underneath.

Go around twice when you stitch up the pocket bag, and use a small stitch (1/16 in [2–2.5 mm]) for extra strength.

2.59 Womenswear jacket with box pleat pockets and flaps.

2.62 Menswear jacket with jetted pockets and large pocket flaps.

2.60 Levi's jeans with trademark pocket.

2.61 Hugo Boss jacket with pleated patch pockets.

2.63 Womenswear jacket with jetted pockets.

# Bias cut

Madeleine Vionnet was the first designer to introduce bias-cut garments successfully. Women exchanged their girdles for bias-cut dresses that draped across their bodies and showed off their natural shape. Bias-cut garments are cut at 45 degrees to the straight grain of the fabric. For more information on fabric grain, see p. 56.

## How to create bias-cut garments

- Choose the right fabric for the garment: crepe, crepe de chine, satin crepe, georgette, silk and chiffon are all perfect for the job.
- Bias-cut garments should be cut on a true bias, 45 degrees from the straight grain of the fabric.
- For the fabric to hang properly, the true bias must run through the center of the panel (center front and center back).
- Some bias cuts depend on the fabric hanging longer on one side; cross grain is not twisted as tight as straight grain and therefore falls more easily on the bias.
- Fabric on the bias moves easily. To control the fabric, use a layer of tissue paper or pattern paper underneath and pin together. Trace the pattern pieces on to a sheet of paper the same size as the fabric and pin all layers together. Use sharp scissors to cut out the pieces.
- Always do some test stitching to find the right machine and stitching type. An overlocking seam works well, as it will allow the seam to stretch.

**2.64 Diane Von Furstenberg, SS16.**

- All garments cut on the bias create fitting problems; therefore, it is important to have fittings in order to reduce excess fabric created by the stretch of the bias. A combination of drafting and draping is essential when working on the bias.
- The best way to fasten a bias-cut garment is with a zip. Use a tape and hand tack the zip first before using the sewing machine.
- It is often best to cut the facings for bias-cut garments on the straight grain and to tape necklines, armhole and shoulders to stop the pieces growing out of shape.
- A pin hem is a nice hem finish. However, if you would prefer a rougher look, use a raw edge.

### Cowls

Cowls are drapes that fall in soft folds off the shoulder point and drape along the front neckline or back. The folds are created using a true bias cut, and the pattern can be constructed on the flat or by draping on a mannequin. Some cowls are designed with pleats or gathers with varying numbers of folds. Cowls can either be cut in one piece with the garment or as a separate piece.

**2.65 Menswear shirt with cowl collar.**

# Fitting the toile

All garments should be properly fitted before going into production, and a number of methods can be employed to do this. When creating bespoke garments, the toile will be fitted on the customer in person. However, designs that are created for a design house or high street store will most likely be fitted on a house model or a mannequin stand.

## Carrying out a fitting

A designer will produce a "toile" for the first fitting. This is a garment made out of a cheaper fabric close in weight and behaviour to the final fabric, such as calico. Calico is a cheap cotton fabric and comes in different weights: lightweight for blouses and shirts; medium for jackets and trousers and heavy for coats or sculptured pieces. A toile has no finished seams, no fastenings, nor any lining or facings.

### Tips for the first fitting

When preparing for a toile fitting, some parts of the garment can be hand sewn, for example, the sleeve into the armhole. The rest of the toile should be sewn together with a bigger machine stitch (⅛ – ³⁄₁₆ in [3–4 mm]), as it is easier to unpick the toile after the fitting if necessary.

Mark all the lines necessary for a fitting; for example, center front and back, waist and hip line, elbow line. These lines can be marked with a pen or thread.

If using shoulder pads, use the same pair as for the final garment. The same applies to any underpinnings such as underskirts and corsetry.

The collar can be fitted without an under-collar attached in the first fitting, as it makes it easier to fit for a better shape.

Pocket positions can be drawn on in the fitting. It is easier to find the right position with the live model, as they can attempt to put his or her hands into the pocket. If pocket flaps or patch pockets are used, cut out shapes of the sample fabric ready to be pinned on in the fitting. If the final fabric has a pattern, draft parts of it onto the toile to show off detailing.

All seams or darts on the toile need to be pressed out really well and in the same order as on the final garment.

At the first fitting, the designer looks at the proportions and fit of the garment. Only once the overall shape has been established does the attention turn to the details. Such details might include the position of pockets, belt loops, collar size and other detailing. These will usually be marked with a tape, marker pen or pinned-on fabric pieces.

A well-fitted garment should complement the design and the body shape. As such, it is best to fit on a live model so that it is possible to see the movement of the garment. The most difficult areas of the body to fit are the armhole and sleeve, the trouser crotch and around the bust area. Before starting with the pattern construction, make sure that you use a well-fitting block to avoid unnecessary fitting problems and always construct your pattern on the large side. It is easier to fit a toile by adjusting the shape to the body than it is to start opening up seams and patching in sample fabric to make it bigger.

The choice of fabric is important, as it needs to reflect the quality of the final fabric used. If working on a woven style, use a calico in the right weight. Again, for jersey/knitwear garments, use a jersey of the right weight. When cutting out the toile, make sure to cut in the right grain line; if the garment is meant to be cut on the bias, then the toile needs to be cut on the bias, too. The different grain lines make the garment drape differently on the body. The toile should always be made out of an unpatterned, light-colored fabric as this shows off the seams and details of the garment in the best possible way.

## Further fittings

Any alterations that have been made since the first fitting will be revisited in the second fitting. The detailing will be looked at and discussed. Decisions about finishes such as binding or top-stitching are finalized. Once everyone is happy with the fit, the garment can be cut out in the final fabric and a shell fitting can take place.

The shell fitting enables the designer to see how the final fabric behaves on the body. As such, the garment is only very basically constructed. The seams are not cleaned up and facings and lining are not yet attached. If necessary, small alterations can still take place at this stage.

Sometimes more than one or two toile fittings take place, especially on new shape developments. Fittings are time-consuming and cost money, but they are necessary for a well-proportioned and well-fitting garment.

**2.66 Christian Dior fitting a house model.**

## Altering the pattern

Alterations are tricky and cannot be
ignored, as a poorly-fitted garment will not
sell. Whether we are tall, short, small or big,
the high street is offering a more diverse
collection to choose from and customers
will not accept a badly fitting outfit.

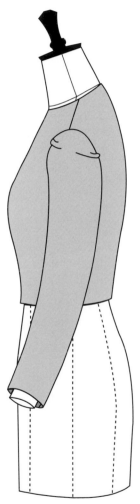

**2.67 The look: the sleeve shows horizontal
lines that pull across the sleeve head, which
look like a pleat.**

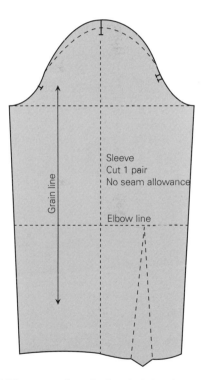

Grain line

Sleeve
Cut 1 pair
No seam allowance

Elbow line

**2.68 The correction: the head of the sleeve
(also called the scye) is too long. Pin across
the sleeve head where the pleat is showing,
or pin away the extra fabric on the top of
the sleeve head/scye. Then correct on the
pattern by folding away the paper in the
same way that the fabric sleeve was pinned.
Re-cut the sleeve and fit it again on a model.**

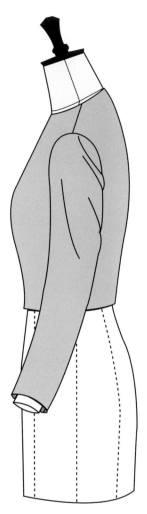

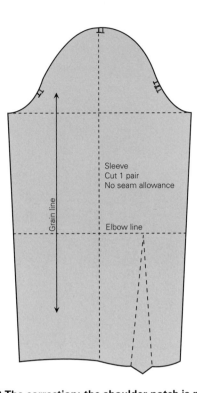

Grain line

Sleeve
Cut 1 pair
No seam allowance

Elbow line

**2.69 The look: the sleeve shows a diagonal pulling from the back to front on the sleeve head area.**

**2.70 The correction: the shoulder notch is not in the right position. The sleeve needs to be turned in by a certain amount, between ³⁄₁₆ in (0.5 cm) and ¹³⁄₁₆ in (2 cm), depending on how much the sleeve is pulling. Change the position of the shoulder notch and try the same sleeve in the armhole using the new shoulder notch as a guide. This is also known as altering the pitch of the sleeve.**

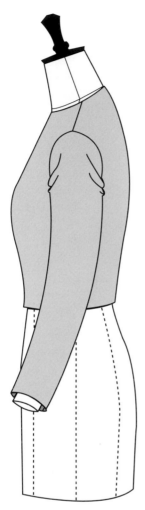

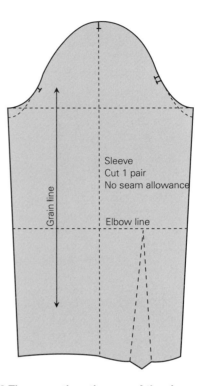

Sleeve
Cut 1 pair
No seam allowance

Elbow line

Grain line

**2.71 The look:** the sleeve shows diagonal pulling from bottom to top at the front and back of the sleeve.

**2.72 The correction:** the scye of the sleeve is too short. By taking fabric from the sleeve head, the sleeve should fit in the armhole. Pin along the scye seam until the sleeve falls straight down from the armhole. Take the amount pinned off the sleeve from the underarm position of the sleeve pattern.

# Laying a pattern on to fabric

It takes time and patience to cut out a pattern in fabric. Taking time to prepare for cutting and marking the fabric pieces guarantees a better result when putting the garment together. It is also helpful to have a firm understanding of fabrics and weaving techniques. For more information on the specific qualities of various fabrics see *Basics Fashion Design: Textiles and Fashion*.

## What is a grain line?

A material is woven using a yarn going lengthways (the warp) and crossways (the weft). The lengthways edge of the fabric is called the selvedge. The cut of a garment in relation to the direction of the grain line will strongly affect how the fabric hangs on the body. There are three ways of cutting the grain:

**Straight grain**—This is the most common method, whereby the grain line of the pattern pieces is parallel to the selvedge. The yarn used lengthways (warp) is a stronger yarn than the one used crossways (weft).

**Cross grain**—This method uses pattern pieces that are cut at a 90-degree angle to the selvedge. Pieces that are cut crossways are most likely to be decorative, for example cuffs, yokes, collars and complex shapes, such as a whole circle skirt.

**Bias**—For a true bias cut, pattern pieces are cut at a 45-degree angle to the selvedge and cross grain. Garments cut on the bias are lively and drape beautifully around the body but will take up a lot more fabric.

Selvedge Edge

Straight grain line runs parallel to the selvedge edge

Weft

Warp
45 degrees to selvedge

Warp

Selvedge Edge

**2.73 The cut of a garment in relation to the direction of the grain line can strongly affect how the fabric hangs on the body.**

## Preparing the fabric

Examine the fabric carefully before cutting out the pattern pieces. There are some elements to watch out for:

### Does the fabric need pressing before cutting?

**Wool:** pure wool (or fabric that contains wool fibers) shrinks and therefore needs to be steamed with an iron before it is cut out.

**Cotton/linen:** fabric from cotton or linen fiber that has not been treated needs to be pressed with steam to shrink it and to press all the creases out before cutting.

**Silk:** silk does not shrink but still benefits from a good press to get rid of the creases. This makes it easier to cut the pattern out. Use a dry iron on silks (without steam).

**Synthetics:** synthetics do not crease much and do not shrink. Press slightly without steam.

### Does the fabric have a direction?

**Nap:** a nap can be on one or both sides of the fabric. The fiber ends stick out on the surface of the fabric, making it soft to the touch. These fabrics, such as velvet, corduroy, fur, or brushed cotton, should be cut in one direction only.

**Shine/color:** some fabrics have a shine or change color when they are looked at from different angles.

### Which are the good and the wrong sides of the fabric?

When buying a fabric from the roll, the good side is usually facing the inside of the roll. If buying a piece of fabric with no clear indication, go with whichever side is preferable or by looking at the selvedge. Any needle holes in the selvedge or marks where the holes have been punched through indicate the wrong side of the fabric.

### Does the fabric have straight edges and does it need straightening out?

Look at the fabric on the table. Some fabrics need to be pulled by hand in both directions to be straightened out. To get a straight crossways line, pull one of the weft threads by hand as a guiding line and cut along the pulled thread.

## Layout of the pattern—cutting plans

### Laying the pattern pieces on the correct grain line

To place the pattern pieces correctly on to the fabric, use the grain line information on your pattern (the long arrow through the pattern). Once you have decided which direction to place the pattern, make sure that the grain line is parallel to the selvedge on the fabric. To ensure that the pattern piece is laid correctly, measure from both ends of the arrow/grain line out to the selvedge.

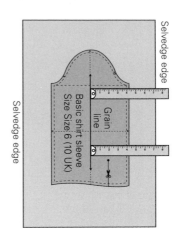

### Double layout

This is the easiest cutting plan of all. The pattern is constructed one side only (one front piece, one sleeve, one back piece, etc.) and indicated with the message "cut 2 x" or "cut a pair." Some pattern pieces are half of a pattern with a folding line and the cutting instruction "cut on fold" (half of collar, half of yoke). The fabric is folded exactly in half by placing one side of the selvedge on to the other side throughout its length. The pattern is then laid on to the fabric as economically as possible. The pieces can be laid in any direction if the fabric has no shine or nap.

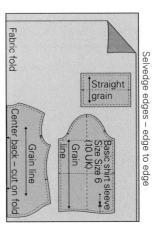

### Single layout

For this layout, the pattern has to be copied open (the whole of the front or back) and indicated with the cutting instruction "cut 1 x or cut 1 self." This cutting plan is used when the pattern pieces are asymmetric or the fabric has a pattern design. The fabric is placed openly with the selvedge to the right and the left running down lengthways. The pattern pieces should be laid in one direction if there is a one-way design on the fabric.

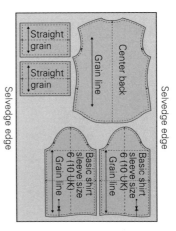

## Layout for fabric with a nap or one-way design

This can be cut out as a single or double layout. Decide on the direction of the nap or design of the fabric and mark the top of the fabric. Then place all the pattern pieces in one direction, running from the top downwards along the selvedge.

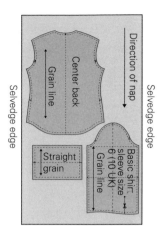

## Crossway layout

This method is used when the pattern pieces are complex shapes and do not fit any other way; for example, a whole circle skirt. Instead of folding the fabric along the long side, the fabric is folded crossways with the selvedge on each side touching. A fabric with nap needs to be cut along its folding line into two pieces. Turn one layer around—wrong side facing wrong side of the fabric—so that the nap runs in the same direction.

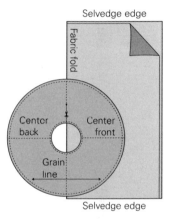

## Cutting out checks and stripes

Before cutting the fabric, ascertain whether or not the check or stripe pattern is symmetrical. You can use the double layout or the single layout when the pattern is symmetrical. When using the double layout, make sure you match up by pinning the checks or stripes together every 4 in (10 cm). This will avoid mismatch of the check or stripe pattern on symmetric pieces such as sleeves and front pieces. It is important that the adjoining pattern pieces match up with the pattern on the fabric. Therefore, mark the dominating bars/stripes on to the pattern and then match up on to the adjoining pattern piece. The parts to watch out for are the side seams, center front and back, armhole and sleeve, pockets, facings, cuffs, yoke and collar.

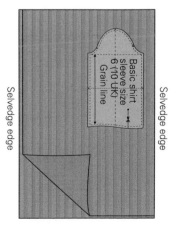

## Marking the pattern onto the fabric

The pattern can be marked on to the fabric once you have decided which cutting plan to use. First, the pattern pieces are weighed down and/or pinned on to the fabric and aligned with the grain line. It is best practice to mark around the paper pattern before lifting it off. This helps to avoid cutting into the paper pattern when cutting the fabric. However, it is essential to transfer all information necessary for constructing the garment on to the fabric pieces. There are different ways to do this:

## Chalk marks

Using a tailor's chalk to mark certain positions such as dart endings and pocket position is easy and not very time consuming, but be careful that the chalk mark cannot be seen on the good side of the fabric.

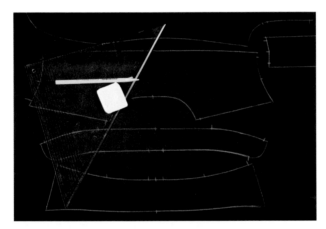

**2.74 Chalk marks.**

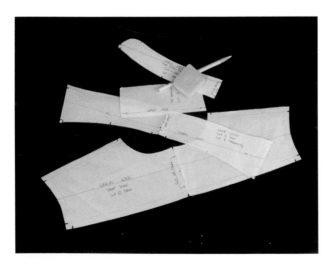

**2.75 Transferring the pattern to fabric.**

## Thread marks

Double the thread in the sewing needle and sew into the fabric to mark the points. This method is used on fabrics that are very thin, delicate or where the tailor's chalk would not show up on the fabric. A thread mark is also a very good way to show positions on the good and wrong side of the fabric at once (chalk marks can only be seen on one side of the fabric). Also, thread marks can be taken out without leaving a trace.

## Laser and hole-punch marking

This method is common in the industry to meet the needs of mass production. For example, the end of a dart position is marked with a hole set 0.2 in (0.5cm) inside the dart. In this way, the hole will not show on the good side of the garment. Punching a needle through layers of fabric or using a laser beam creates a hole-punch effect.

**2.76 Thread marks.**

## Inspired practitioners

### Izumi Harada, Head pattern cutter at Hussein Chalayan

Izumi is the Head Pattern Cutter at Hussein Chalayan and has been working professionally for over 20 years.

**Where did you train?**

I studied at Bunka Fashion College Tokyo Japan. My first job was as a design assistant at Kansai Yamamoto on the show collection line.

Bunka gave me a good technical foundation but really, as a pattern cutter I'm self-trained. I began working professionally at Hussein Chalayan from 1998 starting on special showpieces and then gradually expanding to cover all categories.

**When interpreting a design, do you use a 3D approach or stand?**

If it's a new style, I prefer to drape from scratch rather than using blocks. It gives me a sense of freedom that otherwise I don't have. If you rely too much on pre-existing basic blocks it's harder to generate a completely new silhouette.

**What areas of pattern cutting do you enjoy the most?**

Mainly draping. I really enjoy working from a verbal brief or a very rough sketch. I like the freedom to inject my own feeling into the piece while still trying to respect the mood that the designer wishes to convey.

**What challenges do you face as a pattern cutter?**

Endless challenges. It's what keeps life interesting—working creatively to sometimes impossible deadlines, juggling many projects at the same time whether it's the pre-collection, a dance performance or the show specials. And all the time trying to put your mind into the designer's head to help them get where they are trying to go.

**Does technology help you in your work?**

Technology can make the more laborious processes easy and quick, but in the end, if you want to cut creatively, you need to put your hands on the fabric and feel it.

**Any advice for aspiring pattern cutters or designers?**

It is useful to have a method of pattern cutting, but don't be afraid to break the rules. You only need a few holes or a slash to put a head or an arm through and a piece of fabric becomes clothing. Don't limit yourself because of what a textbook says; be free to make everything.

## Task

### Sleeve exercises

Design three simple garments with varying sleeves, using your blocks as a starting point and methods outlined in this chapter. Keep each design varied to try different methods of pattern cutting.

Suggested starting points:
- A simple bodice with dart manipulation and a gathered sleeve (using the close fitting block)
- An oversized top with a laid on or kimono sleeve (using the overgarment block)
- A dart manipulated top with a raglan sleeve (using the close fitting block)

Pattern cut these three styles. Name, and mark with the correct information ready to be cut out in fabric.

### Collar exercises

Design three simple collars, using the close-fitting block as a starting point. These collars can be inspired by your own research, but bear in mind how they interact with the rest of the garment. Will you need to consider button stands? How will the garment close? Will your neckline have to be altered?

Suggested starting points:
- A flat Peter Pan collar
- A shirt collar with separate stand
- A tailored collar with lapel

Pattern cut these three styles. Name, and mark with the correct information ready to be cut out in fabric.

### Integration

Design one full garment with a choice of collar and sleeve. Think about what this garment is and what you want the overall look to be.

Consider the following:
- Openings (How can you get into the garment?)
- Dart manipulation (to enhance or simplify style lines)
- Design details, such as pockets
- Which grain of fabric best suits your design? (Bias cut, straight of grain)
- How the collar and sleeve work together in your design

Decide which block to use and pattern cut this style labelling it with the correct information ready to cut out in fabric.

### Cutting exercise

Consider what fabric you wish to use and start to cut out your deisgn. Remember to use the correct grain as stated on your pattern pieces and to consider whether you should be cutting out the piece twice or as a pair.

Practice marking the pieces on to your fabric using chalk marks, thread marks or pins. You may want to try different techniques for different styles.

Start to cut out the pieces in the most economical use of the fabric (also known as your lay plan) and keep all the pieces according to style.

# 3

# Garment Construction

This chapter introduces the different tools and machinery used to construct a garment. We will look at the numerous techniques available to hand sew or machine stitch a range of fabrics, and we will take a closer look at the history of haute couture and the tailoring crafts.

Garment construction can be divided into different specialised areas: At the top of the manufacturing chain are haute couture and the tailoring crafts, which involve working with individual customers. At the lower end of the manufacturing chain are industrially produced garments. In contrast to tailoring and haute couture, garments produced in this way are much quicker to manufacture. A lot of the work is mass-produced by machinery and time-efficient construction methods.

This chapter looks at the various tools and materials used to construct garments and provides an introduction to hand sewing and machine sewing techniques.

**3.1 A student at work.**

# Tools for the technique

The following equipment is used in the construction of garments. You will find the necessary items for hand and machine sewing in most haberdashery shops. If you are looking to invest in industrial machinery, then talk to a tradesman first.

**Fabric scissors/shears (1)** Depending on the weight and thickness of the fabric, different kinds of shears can be used. Look for a medium-size pair of scissors for normal use and another larger pair for heavier fabric. It is important that the scissors/shears lie comfortably in your hand, so try them out before buying them. You should always go for the best quality you can afford when buying a cutting tool. To prolong their life, fabric scissors should only be used on fabrics.

**Hand-sewing needles (2)** There is a big variety of sizes, shapes and points to choose from. For most purposes, use a medium-length (1.5 in [37 mm]), thin sewing needle with a round eye.

**Tape measure (3)** You should have one hanging around your neck at all times when sewing together a garment in order to take control measurements throughout the process.

**Embroidery scissors (4)** These scissors are small and sharp with pointed blades. They are good to use for small detail cutting or to snip threads.

**Tailor's chalk (5)** This chalk comes in several colors and can be brushed off after application. There are also wax/synthetic chalks available in white and black. These come off when pressed over by a hot iron.

**Pins (6)** Pins come in different sizes and materials. Stainless steel, 1½ in (35 mm) dressmaking pins are pleasant to handle. When working with knitwear, use safety pins— normal pins will disappear into the garment.

**Machine sewing needles (7)** You will need these in a variety of types and sizes.

**Thimble (8)** A thimble made out of metal is best to protect your fingertip.

## Pressing equipment

**Point pressing block (1)** Good to use on small, sharply-angled areas such as cuffs and collars.

**Needle board (2)** The board has fine needles very close together and is used to press fabrics such as velvet, corduroy and brushed fabrics while protecting the nap or pile.

**Tailor's ham (3)** A firmly stuffed cushion that will help to press round shaped parts or seams on a garment (for example around the bust area).

**Sleeve board (4)** A narrow, padded board for long, straight seams. Perfect to use on a sleeve once the seams are closed down.

## Machinery

**Bobbin and bobbin case (5)** These are used for industrial sewing machines.

**Industrial flat bed machine (6)** This machine can sew any type of fabric using a basic straight stitch.

**Overlocker (7)** Overlocking stitches are used to protect the edges of a fabric. They can be made up of three, four or five threads and the type of fabric dictates which to use. An overlocking stitch is a series of threads that combine to lock the fabric along its edge. A blade runs along the edge of the fabric chopping off excess material and threads.

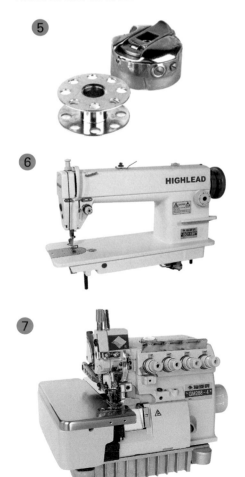

**Sewing machine feet (8)** There are many different types of sewing machine feet including the zip foot for concealed and one/both-sided zips (left), and the universal sewing machine foot (right)

**Coverstitch (9)** A coverstitch machine is used in the construction and finishing of jersey fabrics and for lingerie. Twin needles create two rows of stitching on the right side of the fabric and an interlocked loop on the wrong side. A variation of this stitch creates the interlocked loop on one or both sides of the fabric. Unlike an overlocking machine, this machine does not cut off excess fabric.

**Buttonhole machine** (not shown) This machine creates two kinds of buttonhole: a "keyhole" and a "shirt" buttonhole. Shirt buttonholes are the most common type. Keyhole buttonholes are mainly used on tailored garments, such as coats and suit jackets.

**Industrial iron and vacuum table (10)** An industrial iron is heavier and more durable than a domestic iron, and the steam has a higher pressure. It can be used with a vacuum table, which is shaped like an ironing board and often has a smaller board for ironing sleeves. A pedal underneath the machine allows the user to create a vacuum while ironing; the air and steam are sucked through the fabric into the bed of the machine. This reduces the steam in the atmosphere and also holds the fabric to the ironing board, allowing for easier pressing.

Pressing is essential to a garment; fabric will crease and rumple as it is handled and manipulated under a machine. Unpressed seams do not lie flat, and the garment will look unfinished if it is not ironed.

**Fusing press (11)** A fusing press is the industrial machine used to attach (melt) iron-on interfacing to fabric. It is more efficient and durable than an industrial iron.

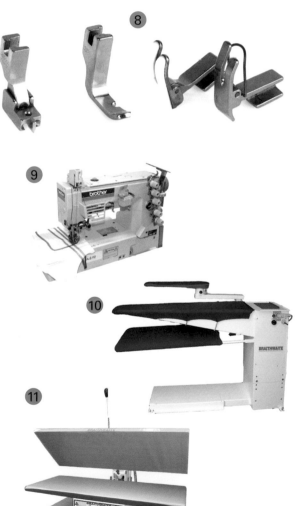

## The right thread for the job

These days, there are threads in all sorts of colors and thicknesses, for all kind of jobs. The material to spin a thread can be natural (cotton or silk) or synthetic, such as polyester. Cotton thread is used primarily for cotton, linen or wool fabric, whilst silk thread is used for silk or woollen fabrics. This is also a beautiful thread for most kinds of hand sewing, as it glides through any type of fabric. The polyester thread can be used for both natural and synthetic fabrics.

### Tacking thread

Tacking thread is a loosely twisted cotton thread that breaks easily. It is used for basting stitch, a temporary stitch that can be removed when it is no longer needed.

**3.2 Thread on cones.**

**3.3 Silk thread on spools.**

**3.4 Cotton thread.**

**3.5 Wool and linen yarn on card.**

**3.6 Metallic thread.**

**3.8 Top-stitching yarn.**

**3.7 Decorative yarn in bundles.**

**3.9 Nylon thread.**

# Seams

Seams are the most basic way of joining two or more pieces of material together in garment construction. Seam allowance is added; this usually faces the inside of a garment but varies according to the type of seam used. Seams are also used to create shape and have an impact on the design of the garment. Some seams are used to strengthen parts of a garment (in corsetry, for example) while others are there simply for design purposes. There are some points to consider when choosing the right seam for constructing a garment. Different fabrics and styles require different seams. You will find various styles of seam to choose from, and it is always possible, of course, to create your own.

### Getting started

The seams introduced here are made using a sewing machine. There are two ways of preparing a seam: One is to place the pieces of material together, using pins to hold them in place. The other (safer) way is to place the material together and hold in place with a hand basting stitch running along the stitching line (see p. 79).

Once the material is ready to be taken under the machine, start the stitching process by taking a couple of stitches forward and then secure the stitching by going back in the same line and forward again, this is known as a back tack. When coming to the end of the seam, repeat by going back a couple of stitches and then forward again. This will secure the sewing line. Also make sure that any hanging threads are neatly cut off before moving on to the next stage.

### Running/plain seam

This kind of seam is the most basic and common version, with seam allowances ranging ³⁄₁₆–1 in (0.5–2.5 cm).

- Place two pieces of material together with the right sides facing and use a basting stitch to hold the seam allowance together.
- Use a flatbed (lockstitch) sewing machine to sew the seam, creating a straight line of stitches.
- The length of the stitch can be changed on the sewing machine from ¹⁄₃₂ in (1 mm) to ³⁄₁₆ in (5 mm) (basic stitch length is ¹⁄₁₆ – ³⁄₈ in [2.5–3 mm]).
- The seam allowance can be overlocked or bound to stop the edge from fraying.
- This seam can be pressed open or to one side.

**3.10 Running seam used to attach two pieces of fabric.**

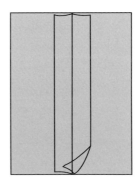

**3.11 Running seam pressed open with an iron.**

**3.12 Overlocked seam allowance pressed open.**

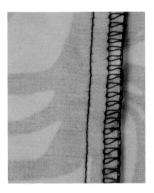

**3.13 Overlocked seam allowance pressed to one side.**

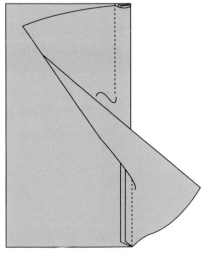

**3.14 Technical drawing of a French seam.**

## French seam

The French seam creates a neat finish and is primarily used for transparent and fine fabrics. It is the favorite of the couture atelier (from where it originated). The seam allowances are cut ½ in (1.2 cm) in total.

- To start, place the wrong sides together. Take a ³⁄₁₆ in (0.5 cm) seam allowance and stitch a seam on the right side of the fabric.
- Then turn the seam inside out, placing the right sides of the fabric together. Stitch the seam, taking a ¼ in (0.7 cm) seam allowance and encasing the previously stitched seam.
- Press the seam to one side.

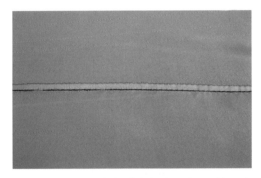

**3.15 Wrong side of the fabric showing a French seam finish.**

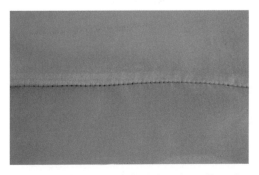

**3.16 Good side of the fabric showing a French seam finish.**

## Flat fell seam

The flat fell seam is popular on denim garments, men's shirts and work wear. It is a hardwearing, strong self-enclosed seam. It shows two rows of stitching on the right side and one row of stitching on the wrong side of the garment. The seam allowance is ¼ in (0.7 cm) on one side and $^{11}/_{16}$ in (1.7 cm) on the other.

- Place the wrong sides of the fabric together. Move the piece with the ¼ in

(0.7 cm) seam allowance ⅜ in (1 cm) further in from the other piece.
- Sew a seam taking the $^{11}/_{16}$ in (1.7 cm) seam allowance from the outer edge.
- Then fold over the ⅜ in (1cm) extra allowance to cover the ¼ in (0.7 cm) allowance and press flat.
- To finish off, top-stitch $^{1}/_{32}$ –$^{1}/_{16}$ in (1–2mm) from the folded edge (edge stitch).

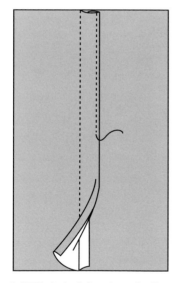

**3.17 Technical drawing of a flat fell seam.**

**3.18 Good side of a flat fell seam on a jeans trouser.**

## Welt seam

A welt seam can be confused with a top-stitched seam, but when looking closer, the seam shows a distinct ridge on one side. The welt seam is one of the strongest seams and is used in garments such as designer tailored wear or denim wear. Depending on the preferred width of the welt cut, the seam allowance is 9/16 in (1.5 cm) for a finished welt width of just under a centimeter.

- Put the right sides together and sew a straight line, taking a 9/16 in (1.5 cm) allowance.
- Press the seam to one side.
- Trim off a couple of millimeters from the enclosed seam allowance.
- With right side up, top-stitch to enclose the trimmed edge.

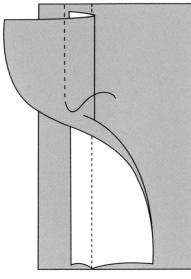

**3.19 Technical drawing of a welt seam.**

# Seam finishes

The raw edge of a seam allowance usually needs treating to stop the fabric from fraying. The technique used to finish a seam allowance depends on the style of garment and the budget. Here are some options to choose from:

1. The easiest and cheapest way to clean up an edge is to overlock the edges using a three or four-thread coverstitch machine.

2. French seams are a seam and seam finish in one. They are more time consuming, and therefore more expensive, but provide a clean way to finish off fine and transparent fabrics.
3. Bound seam allowances are popular on half-lined jackets or jackets without a lining and on trouser seams.

**3.20 Overlocked seam.**

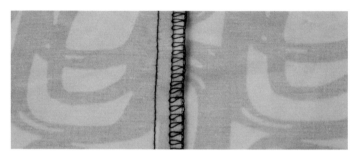

**3.21 French seam.**

**3.22 Center back seam with a bound seam finish.**

## Edge and seam finish with a binding

Any raw edge such as a hem, neckline or seam allowance can be finished with a binding. Bindings are strips of fabric that can be cut to any width. When using a woven fabric as a binding, cut the fabric on the true bias grain line. Bindings are visible on both sides of the garment.

- Prepare the edge by cutting off the allowance (except if you are binding seam allowances).
- Cut a strip off the chosen fabric four times the width of the finished binding.
- Press the binding strip lengthways in half, with the wrong sides together.
- Open the strip up and fold both long sides in to meet the pressed center line and press again.
- Now take the raw seam edge and wrap the binding strip around it and pin in place. The center pressing line of the binding is now aligned with the raw edge of the garment.
- Put it under the sewing machine and top-stitch the binding down at the right side of the garment, through all layers with an edge stitch, catching both binding edges at the same time.

**3.23 Jason Wu, SS16.**

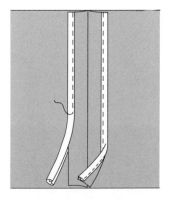

**3.24 Technical drawing of an open pressed seam allowance with bound edges.**

# Hand sewing techniques

Sewing machines are now highly sophisticated and can handle a whole range of very specific sewing tasks. However, there are skilled areas in garment construction which, either by choice or simply because there is no other way, are better addressed with hand sewing. Hand sewing can be relaxing and often helps to create a special bond between you and the garment. It is important to use the right needle and thread and also to use a thimble to protect your finger. Sit on a good chair with a foot rest so you don't have to bend over your work, and do not arch your back too much. Make sure you work in good light. Always sew toward yourself, and do not cut your thread too long, as it gets in knots. Furthermore, do not pull the thread too tight, as this will show on the outside of the garment.

### Getting started

First make sure that the thread has a small knot on the end. Begin your hand sewing with a backstitch. Pick a tiny bit of fabric at the starting point. Pull the thread with the knot through the fabric and do another stitch at the same point to create a loop. Pass the thread back through the loop to secure the knot and prevent it from slipping out.

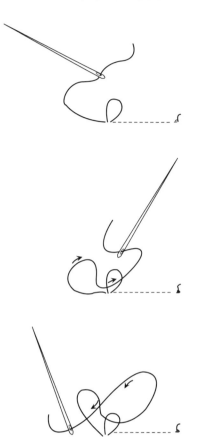

3.25 Technical drawing showing how to secure the thread at the beginning and end of hand stitching.

## Basting stitch

Basting is used to temporarily join together parts of garments. The stitches are large, applied without tension and made using tacking thread in a contrasting color. This process, also known as tacking stitch or running stitch, starts with a larger backstitch without a knot. It is not secured at the end, making the stitches easily removable. Basting is also used to join the edges of two identical pieces of fabric, such as organza and satin-duchess, so the two fabrics can be used as one piece.

## Woven fabric

Blind hemstitch:

- Fold approximately ³⁄₁₆ in (0.5 cm) of the hem edge back and use a blind hemstitch to sew from the inside of the garment.
- Take a thread or two from the outer fabric (make sure that the thread cannot be seen on the outside of the garment) and make a tiny stitch from the hem.
- Space the stitches about ³⁄₈ in (1 cm) apart. The hemming edge can be overlocked for a flat finish.
- The hem can be underpressed (underpressing is using the iron between the hemming and outer fabric). This means that the shiny line that can sometimes appear after pressing will not show through to the outside of the fabric.

**3.26 Lace fabric and organza sewn together with a basting stitch.**

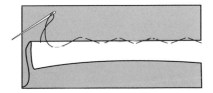

**3.27 Technical drawing of a blind hemstitch.**

## Hemming stitch

Hemming stitches can be used for any kind of hemming (joining two layers of fabric), for example on trouser, sleeve or skirt hems. The stitch is invisible from the outside of the garment and shows very little of the thread on the inside hem.

**3.28 Blind hemstitching on a hemline of a dress.**

### Jersey fabric or knitwear

Jersey and knitwear fabrics have a natural stretch. If it is necessary to finish the hemming lines by hand, make sure that the stitches are not restricting the stretch of the fabric. A cross-stitch hem, also known as a "figure-eight" hem or "catch-stitch" hem, has more stretch than a regular blind-stitch hem and is therefore perfect for use on jerseys and knitwear.

If necessary, the hemming edge can be overlocked before starting the hand stitches.

### Cross-stitching

- Turn the garment inside out and fold the hem allowance over by ³⁄₁₆ in (0.5 cm).
- Work from left to right.
- Secure the hem allowance, then catch one or two threads of the outer fabric.
- Next, take a tiny stitch in the hem and continue the process. Create a crossover with the stitches, leaving ¼ in (0.7 cm) between each one.

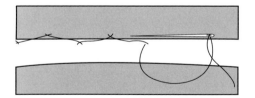

**3.29 Technical drawing of a cross-stitch.**

### Transparent fabrics and silks

To achieve an invisible hem finish, use a roll hem and slip-stitch technique. This kind of hand stitch is common on silk scarves and the cuff openings on blouses made of delicate fabrics, but it can be used on anything that requires a fine edge finish.

- Secure the thread with a knot and a backstitch at the starting point.
- Then turn the edge under by rolling the fabric inwards to the inside (wrong side) of the garment. You will create a tiny roll by doing so.
- Pick a thread from the outer fabric, making sure the thread is not seen on the outside of the garment.
- Then slip the needle directly above it into the turned/rolled edge and through the roll by a couple of millimeters.
- Come out of the roll and take another thread directly below from the outer fabric. Now repeat the process and make sure that no thread is visible from the outside or inside of the garment.
- When rolling the edge over, make sure not to take too much fabric in, as it is a refined finishing method. Using a thin needle and fine thread will make the job easier.

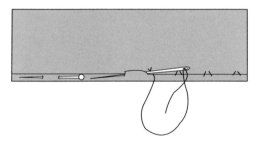

**3.30 Technical drawing of a slip-stitch.**

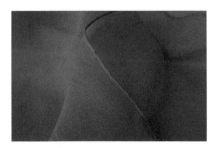

**3.31 Silk scarf with roll hem and slip-stitch finish.**

## Linings

When working on a jacket, attach the hem of the jacket first with a blind hemstitch and then get the lining ready to be attached to the hem. The lining ends about ³⁄₁₆ in (2 cm) above the jacket hem and is cut with extra length for a fold to provide lengthways ease (see "Linings" on p. 176).

Fold the lining ³⁄₈ in (1 cm) over on the hem edge and pin to the jacket hem ³⁄₈ in (1 cm) below its edge. You can use either slip-stitching or prick-stitching to attach the lining.

### Slip-stitching

- Secure your thread at the starting point and catch a small amount of fabric from the jacket hemming only.

- Avoid taking fabric from the outside of the jacket.
- Then immediately at the point of coming out of the fabric, slip into the lining for a couple of millimeters and come out with the needle to catch another small amount of the jacket hem. Continue from right side front to left side front, and remember the jacket is inside out.

### Prick-stitching

- The prick-stitch is similar to the slip-stitch, but it is a stronger version of the two. The difference is that when applying the stitch into the jacket hem, the prick-stitch needs to go back on itself (backstitch) before slipping into the lining.
- This stitch can also be used for sewing in zips.

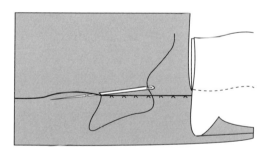

3.32 Use a slip-stitch to attach a lining to a hem.

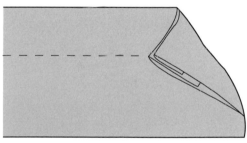

3.33 Lining attached to a hemline of a jacket.

3.34 Technical drawing of a prick-stitch.

3.35 A zip sewn into a dress using prick-stitching.

## Other stitches

Other stitches can be used for decorative effects or to secure weak points on a garment.

### Blanket stitch

- Blanket stitch is a decorative stitch that can also be used to finish a raw edge.
- Choose the depth and length of your stitch and insert the needle vertically, keeping the same distance and depth throughout.
- Working from left to right, pass the needle through from back to front and bring the needle through the thread loop.
- Make sure that the knot lies on the top of the fabric edge.

**3.36 Using a blanket stitch technique as a decorative edge finish on a wool fabric.**

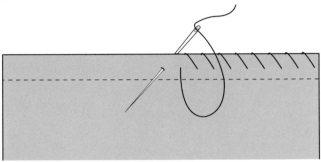

**3.37 An overcast stitch.**

### Overcast stitch

- Overcast stitch is used to finish a raw edge.
- Work from right to left.
- Push the needle through the fabric edge from the back to the front, taking a 1/16 – 1/8 in (2–3 mm) stitch.
- Take the needle pointing left and create slanting stitches of the same distance and depth over the fabric edge.

**3.38 Wool fabric with overcast stitch to prevent the raw edge from fraying.**

## Arrowhead tack

Specific stitches are used to secure a weak point on a garment. Use an "arrowhead" or "cow's-foot tack" for example, to reinforce parts that may be under a lot of strain such as a split in a skirt, the ends of a pocket or the tops of pleats.

- Mark the position of the triangle with thread or chalk. Use a buttonhole thread and secure the thread with a knot.
- Starting on the lower left corner, push the needle through from the wrong side to the right side.

- Working on the right side of the fabric, tack the needle through the top point of the triangle, taking a tiny stitch.
- Then take the needle to the lower right corner and complete a stitch from the lower right corner to the lower left again.
- Continue this process from right to left, with stitches close together, until the triangle is complete.

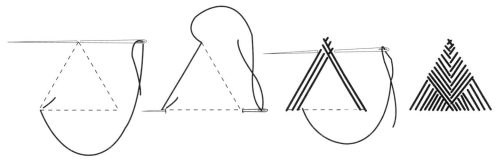

**3.39 An arrowhead tack.**

## Fagotting stitches

Some decorative hand stitches can be used to join two fabric edges together, such as the "fagotted seam." This is an embroidery stitch that creates an open, lacy effect.

- Start by drawing parallel lines on a piece of paper in the desired width of the fagotting.

- Turn both sides of the adjoining raw edge under. Tack these two edges on to the paper lines.
- Then start fagotting the two edges together by taking slanted stitches from one side to the other and pass the needle under each slanting thread to create a crossover.

**3.40 A fagotting stitch.**

**3.41 A version of a hand-sewn fagotting stitch used as an edge finishing.**

## Inspired practitioners
### Sharon Stokes, Sample Maker

Sharon is a sample maker and machinist whose clients include Giles Deacon and Rapha. She is an extremely talented and well respected machinist in the industry and has been working professionally for over 25 years.

**What has your journey been like to your position now?**

It's been quite varied. I studied fashion for four years until 1987. Since then I've been mostly self-employed. The majority of this time has been as a sample machinist, but I also cut patterns from time to time, and for five years I did womenswear garment technology for high street suppliers.

**How important is the construction process in fashion design?**

To me, it's vital. The construction can mean success or failure of a garment. (So can the design, pattern, cloth and cutting, of course). The wrong seam, for example, can alter how a piece hangs, looks, feels and performs. A French seam can be a lovely clean finish on chiffon, for example, but in the wrong cloth and in the wrong place can make a garment look bulky and overworked.

**How much time do you spend experimenting in your work?**

It depends on what project I'm working on. It can be a couple of hours to a couple of days. It's so varied.

I've worked for Giles Deacon for about ten years, and there are fabrics we use season after season that we no longer need to experiment on finishes because we know exactly how these will perform and what type of styles they work well in.

**What difficulties have you had to overcome to really perfect your skill?**

It took years for me to get to the point where I can look at a piece of fabric and see in my mind's eye how it will look when it's made into a garment, what type of construction will work and how it will hang on different grainlines. This has proved to be a very useful skill.

**Any advice for aspiring designers and makers?**

Designers: Keep drawing. Go to exhibitions and take inspiration from everywhere, not just other designers. Architecture and the natural world for example.

Makers: If you really want to make, then have a sewing machine permanently set up. There's much more chance you'll use the machine than if it's shut away in a cupboard somewhere.

You don't have to start by making a complete garment. Make little examples of finishes and details and file them for future reference.

Learn to enjoy unpicking. It's likely you'll be doing a lot of it, but don't let any little mistakes get you down. Mistakes are fine if you learn from them.

Look inside garments and try and figure out how they've been constructed and in what order.

## Task

### Sewing exercises

Compile a sewing book of samples of different seams. Work with a simple fabric like calico or muslin and try the following:
- Running/plain seam
- French seam
- Flat fell seam
- Welt seam

### Finishing exercises

Compile a finish book of different finishing techniques. Work with a simple fabric like calico or muslin and try the following:
- Overlocking a seam open and closed
- Binding a seam together and open
- Pin hemming
- Twin needle coverstitch

### Stitching up a garment

Stitch up the garments that you have cut out in fabric (see p. 63).

Consider the following:
- What kind of seams will this garment have?
- Is this garment lined?
- What kinds of finishings will this garment have, and does this change the overall design of the garment?
- What is your order of make?

**Tips for finishings**

Carefully think about which pieces are joining to which and their steps in the making process. Think about if your finishings need to be done before or after the garment is constructed and how you are attaching sleeves and collars. Some parts may have to be hand finished. Remember to press your seams as you go to ensure a clean and accurate finish and sew.

# Surface-Specific
# Techniques

This chapter deals specifically with the range of
techniques used for specialist fabrics and materials.
Finishes and treatments that are added to a fabric at
any stage of its process can make the material difficult
to cut, sew or finish. These include felted wools, lace,
sequinned and beaded fabrics, knits and fabrics that have
a nap, such as velvet. A material such as fur or leather,
whether it is real or synthetic, also requires specialist
knowledge in its construction.

**4.1 Ashish, SS15.**

# Felted fabrics

Felted woven fabrics are shrunk and compressed with heat, moisture and friction to produce a dense appearance. Some of the better-known felted fabrics are loden, melton or fleece. The edges of a felted fabric do not fray, so seams can be left unfinished. It is most common to use a plain stitched seam with top-stitching or a welt seam for light- to medium-weight felted fabric. But there are many more techniques to choose from, such as the following:

## Abutted seam

Abutted seams (or channel seams) can be used as decorative seams, by applying a ribbon or any contrast fabric as an under layer.

- Prepare a 1³⁄₁₆ in (3 cm) strip as an under layer and mark the center of the strip. You can use contrasting or matching fabric.
- Place the raw edge of both sides of the garment pieces on to the center line of the strip. The strip is lying on the wrong side of the fabric pieces with the right side up.
- Now top-stitch each side of the garment pieces on to the strip.
- If required, you can also leave a gap to show more of the decorative strip.

## Top-stitched hem

The best way to finish a felted fabric garment is with a top-stitched hem, but you could also use a blanket stitch, which creates a certain look and finishes off the edge.

- Add allowance for a hem.
- Turn the hem allowance to the wrong side of the garment.
- Top-stitch the hem down. This can be done at any width, stitch length and row position depending on the design choice. Use any type of thread (color or thickness) or use decorative stitching.

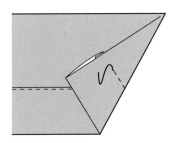

**4.3 A top-stitched hem finish.**

**4.4 A top-stitched hem with ³⁄₈ in (1 cm) turned under.**

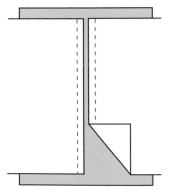

**4.2 An abutted seam.**

## Non-woven flat fell seam

A variation of the flat fell seam is strong enough for non-woven felted fabrics.

- Allow ⁹⁄₁₆ in (1.5 cm) for the seam allowance.
- Put the wrong sides together and sew a straight line.
- Press the seam flat to one side.
- From the inner layer trim off ¹⁄₁₆–⅛ in (2–3 mm).
- Top-stitch the top layer down along the edge.
- To strengthen the seams use a fusible web before top-stitching.

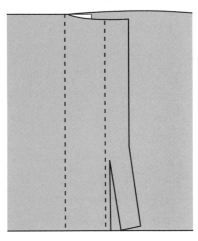

**4.5 A flat fell seam.**

**4.6 Jil Sander AW16.**

# Lace

Lace is a decorative fabric with an open structure. It is made by hand or machine using knitting, braiding, looping and knotting techniques. Lace is used for trimming on lingerie, collars and cuffs or as appliqué, traditionally on bridal or evening wear. It can be fine- to heavyweight, in different fibers such as linen, wool, cotton, polyester or nylon and has more stretch in the width than in the length. Lace is fragile and needs to be handled with care. It is also expensive. You will require more fabric when cutting out because most lace fabrics have a horizontal or vertical pattern that should be matched up, both for garment construction and for trimmings.

**4.7 Celine SS16.**

## Appliqué seams

Appliqué seams are used on lace garments to ensure that none of the side or center back seams are visible.

- Cut the pattern as usual.
- Place the pattern right-side up on to the lace. Lay out the pieces, leaving space between them, aligning the pattern design of the fabric from front side seam to back side seam.
- Be careful with the center front and center back when placing the pieces for a central pattern.
- First thread mark the original side seams of the pattern on to the lace fabric.
- Then thread mark the overlapping pattern on to the front panel.
- Cut the overlapping piece (front piece) following the pattern and add some allowance (this can be cut off later).
- Then cut the back piece (this is the corresponding under layer) with a ⅜ in (1 cm) allowance.
- Put the overlapping layer on top (right-side up) and pin the thread-marked front and back side seam lines together.
- Baste the new side seam and check the fit for small alterations before sewing the pieces permanently together.
- Appliqué around the lace pattern with a small zigzag stitch, either by hand or with the sewing machine.
- Trim all excess allowances off each layer and press the seams carefully at a low temperature.

### Appliquéd lace edging and set-in lace pieces

When integrating lace pieces into a garment or finishing, such as on lace-trimmed necklines or hemlines, great care has to be applied to make the fabric and lace look like a single piece. Lace application should not look like an afterthought but as though it is part of the fabric.

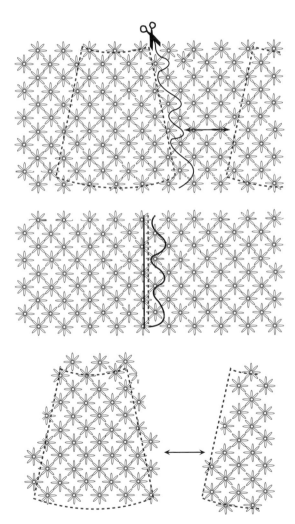

**4.8 Technical drawing showing how to cut lace fabric and create an appliqué seam.**

# Leather

Leather is one of the oldest materials used to cover up the human body. It is not a type of fabric but the skin of a mammal or reptile and is therefore sold by the skin and not by the meter. The hair of the skin is removed, and the grain revealed by a process called tanning (leather can be tanned using several products including: tannin, chrome, alum or oil). The skin will go through a finishing process after the tanning to apply color or a different surface: for example, shiny or matte. It is called leather when the outside of the skin is tanned and finished and known as suede when the inside is finished.

## Sewing leather

Leather does not fray and therefore the edges do not have to be finished. When sewing leather, use a special leather needle and do not pin the skin as it leaves marks. Also, the garment cannot be let out, as it will show the stitches. Leather is sensitive to heat from the iron and may get stained and creased permanently. When working with suede, watch out for the nap.

A leather or suede garment requires a different approach in its construction compared to one made in fabric. To avoid disappointment, always experiment with scraps of leather first, trying out seams and other areas that can cause problems.

- Use a polyester thread (or if the leather is heavy then try a top-stitching thread, which is thicker than a normal stitching thread). Do not use cotton or cotton-wrapped polyester thread, as the treatment used on leather or suede will make the thread rot.
- Start by trying a universal machine needle first. If it skips stitches, use a leather needle that is wedge pointed.
- Use a Teflon foot, roller or leather foot on the sewing machine. The foot may leave marks on the leather, so try first on a scrap of leather.
- For some thicker leathers, a "walking foot" machine can be used. This is

where the foot and the bed of the machine work together to "walk" the leather through the machine.

**4.9 Leather hand-sewing needles and leather machine needles with a wedge point.**

**4.10 Welt seam on leather sample.**

**4.11 Leather seam with top-stitch.**

## Seams for leather

Always consider the weight and style of garment when choosing the seam type. A plain seam works for all thin-to-medium-weight leathers. For the heavier range of leathers, use a lapped seam, as it will create less bulk. Other types of seams are the plain leather seam, slot seam, welt seam or, for extra stability and reinforcement, the taped seam.

- Instead of ironing the seams, these are pressed down or pounded with a cloth-covered hammer.
- Glue (use leather glue, which is more flexible) or top-stitch the seams down to keep them flat. Skive the edges off the seams to avoid bulk.
- Darts are stitched to the dart point, then slashed open and glued or top-stitched down.

**4.12 Leather seam with tape for reinforcement.**

**4.13 Glue and brush to hold down leather seam allowance and hemlines.**

## Hems for leather

To achieve a flat hem on curved edges, cut out triangular notches.

- Hemlines can be glued or top-stitched. Pound the hemline first to get a fold line, then glue or top-stitch close to the fold lines. This is especially important when applying a lining so that the hem edge is left free, allowing you to machine stitch the lining to it.
- For heavier leather, use the raw edge facing. If the leather is nice inside, why not finish off the hemming by turning the hem inside out (wrong-side-out hcm)?

## Fastenings for leather

Suitable fastenings for leather garments are zips of all kinds and bound, slash-stitched buttonholes or buttons with loops. Hook-and-loop fastenings and lacings can also work well. When sewing on the buttons and hooks, use a leather needle and a waxed thread. Apply a small button as a stay button on the facing side.

**4.14 Leather jacket by D&G, Dolce and Gabbana, S/S08.**

# Fur

Real fur, like leather, comes from an animal but with the hair still attached. All real furs have dense short hairs called "under fur" and longer, softer hairs called "guard hairs." Real fur is very expensive to buy and, because of where it comes from, in many countries is unpopular to wear. However, manufactured imitations are becoming more sophisticated. Fake fur fabric is easier to cut, as it comes on the meter and not in skins. It is also easier to sew. The quality can be so good that it is often mistaken for real fur.

Real fur can be processed to make it softer and it can be bleached, dyed or stencilled to change its color. It can also be sheared or curled to give it a different texture and look.

## Sewing fur

A number of methods can be employed to make working with fur easier.

- Use a polyester thread for real fur and any type of thread for fur fabric, as long as the thread is strong enough.
- For real fur, start by trying a universal machine needle. If it skips stitches, use a wedge-pointed leather needle. For woven fur fabrics, a universal machine needle should work well.
- For real fur, use a Teflon foot, roller or leather foot on the sewing machine and a standard machine foot for fur fabric.

### Tips for working with fur

- Fur has a nap and sometimes looks livelier when cut upside down.
- When cutting real or fake fur, make sure to cut the skin only and not the hair. Mark your pattern pieces on the skin side and slide a razor blade, mat knife or scissors carefully through just the skin.

## Plain seam

To avoid the fur hair being caught in the seam, push the pile towards the garment, then stitch the seam and turn around to the fur side. To release fur pile caught in a seam, use a pin and carefully pull the pile out. Also trim away the pile in the seam allowance to avoid extra bulk.

- Fake fur fabric can be carefully pressed with a low-temperature iron on the wrong side. If seams do not lay flat on a real fur garment, then use hand stitching to flatten the seams down.
- The best way to hem a fur garment is to tape it or face it with leather.
- To fasten a fur garment, use faced and inseamed buttonholes, leather button loops, covered hooks and eyes, or simply wrap the front and close with a leather belt. Zips should only be used on short-haired fur, as long-haired furs will get caught in between the zip teeth.

**4.15 Fendi, haute couture AW15.**

# Knits and stretch-woven fabrics

Linking one or more yarns into a series of interlocking loops makes up a knit fabric. Horizontal rows of knit are known as "courses" and vertical rows are known as "wales." Knitted and stretch-woven fabric is comfortable because of its stretchiness. However, care must be taken when working with these fabrics, as pressing and heat can cause the fabric to lose its shape.

## Types of knitted and stretch-woven fabric

There are two types of knitted fabric: one is the weft knit, which is one continuous yarn. This is used to produce fabrics such as jersey, ribbing, sweatshirt knits, inter-locks and double knit. The second is the warp knit, which uses many yarns and one stitch (warp) to produce fabric that is flat with straight edges (jersey, on the other hand, is less stable, runs easily and curls at all cut edges). The best-known warp knit is tricot, which is used, for example, in lingerie. Another is the raschel knit, which has a lacy, openwork appearance. Weft and warp knits use only four basic stitches: plain, rib, purl and warp.

**4.16 Five-thread overlocked side seam of a t-shirt.**

Stretch-woven fabrics must have at least twenty percent stretch in either direction; lengthwise or crosswise. These fabrics can be made with textured yarn, either curled or crimped. They can be given a special finish or woven with yarns made from elastomers (elastomer is a synthetic material that has extensibility and complete elastic recovery). Some well-known stretch fibers are Spandex or Lycra. They can be mixed with cotton, wool or any synthetic fibers. Any traditional fabric such as corduroy, denim, satin or lace can be combined with stretch yarns and therefore gain the characteristic of knits, such as comfort, wrinkle-resistance and a better fit.

**4.17 Coverstitch with two- and three-needle effects on a hemline.**

**4.18 Bound neckline of a t-shirt with coverstitching.**

## Sewing knitted and stretch-woven fabric

Due to its fragile nature, knitted and stretch-woven fabric requires some specific construction methods.

- Use a polyester or cottonwrapped polyester, woolly nylon or elasticated thread.
- Try a universal machine needle for stretch-woven fabrics, and if it skips use a ballpoint and/or stretch needle. It may also be worth trying twin needles.
- Seams can be put together using specialist machinery such as the coverstitch or five-thread overlocker, which will allow the stretch-woven fabric or knit to stretch.
- The hem finishing, like the seams, depends on the style of the garment. You can choose from a variety of hand and machine finishings. For example, if you are working by hand, use a cross-stitch, which will give the stretch needed in the hemming. If you are working on a machine, use a coverstitch with twin needle effects or a zigzag stitch. Applying a binding or ribbon to finish off the edge works well, or try

elastic casing and elastic lace or any other elastic tape. A clean cut raw edge also looks interesting if it does not allow the knit to run.
- When cutting out, make sure you allow the fabric to relax on the table and don't stretch it at any point of the cutting process. Also use fine pins and very sharp scissors.
- Be careful when pressing stretch-woven fabrics and knits, as neither will take a hot iron. When pressing, steam on to the seam and afterwards press down the seam with the fingers.
- Fastenings on knit and stretch-woven fabrics are tricky. Always use an interlining or tapes to restrict the part where the fastening is placed. For example, use a decorative non-stretch tape on the outside or inside of the button stand position. This will keep the garment closed and prevent it from stretching into a different size. Zips, Velcro or magnetic closings can also be used as fastenings.

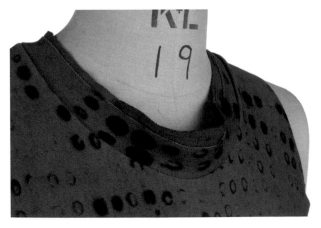

**4.19 T-shirt by Courtney McWilliams with a raw edge finish on the neckline.**

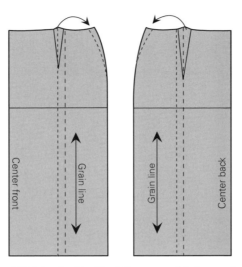

**4.20 A basic skirt block for woven fabrics can be reduced to a jersey skirt block by taking in the skirt to allow for the stretch.**

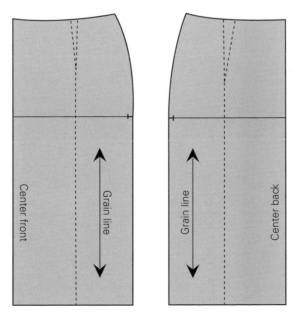

**4.21 The final stretch/jersey skirt block.**

# Sequinned and beaded fabrics

Sequinned and beaded fabrics are glamorous and in the past have been used mainly for eveningwear and special occasions. It is now much more common to use these fabrics for daywear. Sequins, beads and other sparkling stones are sewn or glued on to an underlayer of fabric such as chiffon, satin, taffeta or knits.

## Sewing sequinned and beaded fabric

These fabrics are not easy to handle and extra time and care need to be considered when using them.

- Beads and sequins are applied to the fabric with repeated chain stitch. This means that if pulled from one side, it will unravel badly.
- The best thread to use is polyester or cotton-wrapped polyester for both hand and machine sewing.
- Use a universal machine needle and a hand-sewing beading needle. When using the sewing machine, tack the stitch size down to ⅛ in (2.5 mm).
- If required, you can also leave a gap to show more of the decorative strip.

### Tips for working with sequinned and beaded fabric

- Sequinned fabrics can be uncomfortable on bare skin, therefore the garment should be lined.
- Some sequinned and beaded fabrics can have a pattern and will therefore need matching up. The fabrics usually have a nap/direction and should be cut from a single layer. Make sure to use old but sharp scissors, as the fabric dulls scissor blades.
- Avoid darts and add flare through slash and spread rather than gathers and pleats. Simple sleeve solutions like the kimono or raglan show off the fabric better than a set-in sleeve. Try not to break up the fabric design unnecessarily.
- Before purchasing a sequinned fabric check the width, because most are very narrow (45 in [114 cm]).

## Assembling sequinned and beaded fabric garments

These fabrics are used to their best advantage by employing a simple style with a minimum of seams.

- The seams to use are a plain seam, a double-stitched seam (two close rows of straight stitch lines), a hairline seam (two close rows of straight stitch and zigzag stitch lines) or you can used a taped seam for reinforcement.
- When the garment pieces are cut, take away the sequins along the seams. Only sew the underlayer of fabric together, do not sew through sequins.

- Once the seams are closed, add the missing sequins along the seam line by hand (this will make the seam disappear) and also secure the loose ones around the seam. The same procedure should be used with a beaded fabric.
- Facing and hemming can be done by using tapes, bands, bindings, ribbing or any fabric/lining facings.
- Another way of finishing hemlines is to superlock the edges. Superlock is a very fine and tight overlocking stitch.
- Depending on the style of garment, use a light zip, hook and eye, or loops and buttons to fasten.

**4.22 Ashish AW13.**

# Velvet

Napped or pile fabrics go through a process called "napping," whereby fiber ends are raised to the surface to be either clipped, brushed flat or left standing up. This process can be applied on one or both sides of woven or knitted fabrics.

Pile fabrics are woven with an extra set of yarn. Velvet is a popular fabric of the napped or pile family. Originally velvet was made from silk yarns. Today velvets range from light- to heavyweight and can be woven from cotton, rayon or polyester. Velvet has an extra set of warp yarns and is woven as two layers of fabric. The pile, which joins the layers together, is cut after the fabric is woven. The result is a much denser pile, giving the fabric a rich texture.

## Sewing velvet

Care needs to be taken with velvet once it has been cut, as the pile frays badly at its raw edges. Ironing and pressing velvet can also damage the fabric by flattening the pile, so try to press on the inside of the garment or use a velvet board to avoid using too much pressure. Some other tips for sewing velvet include:

- Use a universal machine needle and take the pressure off the sewing foot. Try using a roller or even-feed machine foot or a zipper foot.

- When sewing seams, make sure you hand tack the seams together as velvet creeps badly and sometimes puckers during the sewing process. You can use a plain seam or tape your seams for extra stability.
- Hemming can be sewn by hand with blind hemstitching or faced with a lighter fabric by machine.
- Clean up frayed edges on seams by binding or overlocking the seam allowance.

**4.23 Emilio de la Morena AW14.**

# Transparent fabrics

Transparent fabrics range from crisp to soft and light- to heavyweight. The best-known crisp, semi-transparent to transparent fabrics are organza and organdie made from silk, cotton or synthetics, as well as marquisette and handkerchief linen. These beautiful types of fabrics are easier to cut and sew than the soft transparent ones. The most common types of soft, semi-transparent and transparent fabrics are chiffon, Georgette and crepe chiffon. These fabrics are so lightweight they are tricky to cut and difficult to sew. You will also find fabrics that you can categorise in between crisp and soft such as voile, batiste, shirtings or gauze. These fabrics might be difficult to work with but are worth all the effort, as they are stunning to look at and delightful to wear.

**4.24 1 Chiffon dress by Yuki with French seam finish and a pin hem.**

## Sewing transparent fabrics

It is worth noting that the softer the fabric, the more time and space you will need to work with it.

- Use a fine (60–70) universal machine needle and reduce the stitch length to $\frac{1}{16}$ in (1.25–2mm), which is a very small stitch.
- Match the thread to the fabric and use a fine to extra fine polyester thread or mercerised cotton.
- Iron all the creases out of the fabric with a dry iron.
- Pin the fabric carefully on to a piece of thin paper the same size as the fabric. The paper is supposed to stop the fabric from moving around, as it is famously slippery.
- After securing the fabric to the paper, add a third layer of paper with the pattern pieces copied on to it. Pin all three layers together and cut out with sharp scissors.
- Make sure that all marks within the pattern piece are thread marked (use a fine needle and extra fine thread). Do not use chalk marks, which will show permanently on the good side of the fabric.
- Carefully clean up the inside of the garment, as the transparent fabric shows all kinds of hems, seams and facings on the outside of the garment. There are several methods you can use for the seams, for example French seams or bindings. The best method for hemming a chiffon garment is a pin-hem and if you work on a budget use a superlock as a finishing. Slip-stitch is a nice hand sewing stitch for hem or edge finishings.
- When it comes to pressing the fabric, consider the material and always try first on a scrap piece. Sometimes using a dry iron makes the fabric static. If this happens, use an antistatic spray.

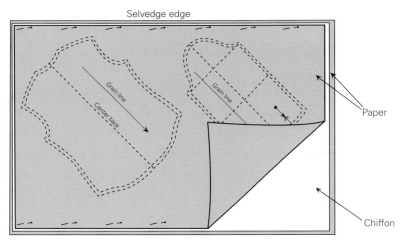

Selvedge edge

Paper

Center back

Grain line

Grain line

Chiffon

Selvedge Edge

**4.25 Example of a layout for cutting fine fabrics.**

**4.26 Example of a pin hem finish on a sleeve hemline.**

**4.27 Sample of a superlock finish.**

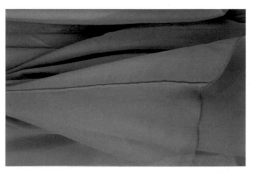

**4.28 Close-up of the French seam finish on the dress by Yuki.**

## Inspired practitioners

### Thomas Tait, Womenswear Designer, Creative Director

Thomas is a womenswear designer and Creative Director. He was the youngest ever student to complete the prestigious Central Saint Martins' Fashion MA under Louise Wilson and is the head of his eponymous womenswear label. Over the years he has received the British Fashion Council's NEWGEN and London's Centre for Fashion Enterprise sponsorship, and in 2014 won the inaugural LVMH Young Designer Prize.

**Where did you train?**
2008 DEC LaSalle College, Montreal Canada

2010 MA Fashion, Central Saint Martins, London UK

**What drives your aesthetic?**
My personal life, fascination with garment construction and luxury goods. My process tends to be quite instinctive and often relates to an idea of how I would like the clothing to feel and how they might influence the psychology of the wearer.

**How important is the construction process in what you design?**
Extremely important. Product development tends to take roughly eighty percent of the design process time.

**Being a womenswear designer, how key is femininity in your work?**
It is very important. As a man, I understand that my perception of femininity and understanding of a woman is unique to me. The gap between myself and the woman I design for is often bridged with a creative freedom that is uniquely my own, and reflects an admiration, fascination and occasional jealousy for the female gender.

**How do you approach experimental pattern cutting?**
I was trained formally at a college in Canada. I excelled most in 3D pattern cutting/draping. What followed was a free development of pattern cutting through the years of further education and building my own collection with a small team of pattern cutters and studio assistants.

I tend to work on reduction of seam, eliminating points of connection in garments with the aim of enveloping the body. This is often mistaken for an origami style of work; in fact, I tend to mold single pieces of fabric or material rather than folding them.

**How do you utilise fabric manipulation and surface embellishment?**
It really depends on the pieces and collection. I have usually applied print processes to manipulate the surface texture of the raw materials. Most recently, I have been fascinated by Boro, a Japanese tradition of recycling found or salvaged materials. This has lead me to work with various methods of washing, quilting and printing to create something that feels at once aged, delicate and futuristic.

**What advice would you give an aspiring designer?**
Find out what it is that speaks most about your personal passions and never lose sight of what is unique to you as a designer. Trust your instincts and never be shy to ask for help.

## Task
### Specialist fabric sewing

1. Explore the following specialist fabrics. Compile a sewing book of samples of different seams and finishings:
   - Felted wool
   - Lace and appliqué
   - Leather
   - Fur
   - Jersey
   - Sequined fabric
   - Velvet
   - Transparent fabrics (chiffon, organza etc.)

   Sample different ways of finishing these fabrics, and how they attach together. Try and experiment with low-profile and low-bulk seaming to give you a clean finish.
2. Start to attach different fabrics together. For example, this might be sewing together sequined fabric with fur fabric. Consider the following:
   - How do these fabrics react next to each other?
   - What different seams might you have to use?
   - What machinery is best for the job?
   - Do you have the right machine feet to handle the fabric?
   - Can this fabric steam or press?

### Manipulating fabrics

Fabric manipulation is an important way of changing the feel of fabric. There are many techniques that can be tried using just a needle and thread. Many manipulating techniques have evolved over the years with techniques being passed down from generation to generation with regional differences.

Some of these techniques include: pleating, tucking, gathering, smocking, shirring and quilting.

By using these techniques, you can transform flat cloth into some dramatic shapes and textures.

Using various fabrics, test out different techniques of manipulation. Try the following:
- Pleating (knife, box, wrinkled, sunray, accordion)
- Gathering (one edge, double edge)
- Tucking (pin, graduated, tapered)
- Smocking
- Shirring (hand and using shirring elastic on the bobbin)

**4.29–4.31 Examples of fabric manipulation and specialist fabrics.**

# 5

# Haute Couture and Tailoring

At the top of the garment manufacturing chain are haute couture and the tailoring crafts, which involve working with individual customers. The garments are constructed using traditional methods such as hand sewing and intricate cuts. The fabric and finishing can often heavily influence the designing process, and the designs will often work to ensure that they are displayed to their best advantage on the body.

A lot of time, consideration and energy is put into a couture or tailored garment. The result is a garment that fits flawlessly, using the finest luxury fabrics, put together with skillful hands by dressmakers and tailors who are proud of their work and the name they work for. To be working as a tailor on Savile Row, for example, or in an atelier for an haute couture house conveys the feeling of exclusivity through history and tradition.

**5.1 Viktor & Rolf, haute couture AW15.**

# Haute couture

Translated literally from French into English, the phrase "haute couture" means "sewing at a high level." Couturiers use only the finest and most luxurious fabrics. Sometimes these have been custom made. A couture garment is meant to fit flawlessly as a result of many fittings and will include perfectly designed proportions for the individual client. Adjustments are made on garments to balance the body shape of the customer. These can include changes to the collar, the proportions of the pockets (one can be slightly bigger than the other), shoulder seams (one can be narrower than the other), or padding in one shoulder to make it higher than the other. For a full figure, all horizontal seam lines are adjusted—not just the waist and hemline. This attention to detail is the essence of haute couture. With the help of the toile, every design detail is planned so that any motifs, stripes or checks are matched and positioned to the best advantage for the client's figure. At garment openings a motif will match so perfectly you have to look twice to discover the fastening. On suits and two-piece designs, the fabric pattern continues uninterrupted from neck to hem.

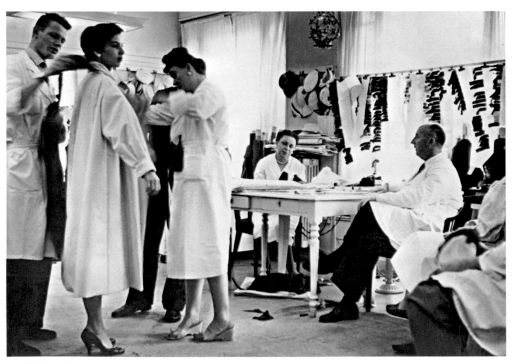

**5.2 Fitting of a coat by Dior, 1956.**

## The history

The origins of haute couture lie in the eighteenth century, with many attributing its birth to the couturier, Rose Bertin (the milliner to Marie Antoinette) and Charles Frederick Worth. Prior to this, clothing would have been made by the couturier to the specifications of the customer. It was not until the mid-nineteenth century that Charles Frederick Worth, who was originally from England, first introduced his customers to garments made up from his own ideas. He showed his collection of finished designs on live models—a novel exercise at the time. He achieved colossal success and opened up a new direction in fashion. Once the customer had selected an outfit from the portfolio (today called a look-book) and specified the color and fabric, the outfit would be made to measure in the atelier (workshop). This is still common practice.

In France, haute couture is a protected name and can only be used by companies that work to a certain standard, as defined by the *Chambre de commerce et d'industrie de Paris*. The rules that define those design houses allowed to become an haute couture label were established in 1945 but have since been updated. To become a member of the *Chambre Syndicale de la Haute Couture* and to be able to use the term *haute couture* in its label

and advertising or in any other way, a design house must follow three main regulations: to provide an atelier in Paris that employs at least fifteen people full-time; to present a collection with at least thirty-five outfits, including day- and eveningwear, to the Paris press; and to provide a service to private clients with bespoke designed garments.

Across Europe, the term *couture* has been used loosely to describe tailor-made and high fashion garments, which can lead to confusion for customers. A collection of garments produced more than once and to a size range is called *prêt-à-porter*, the French term for "ready to wear." As they struggle with their vast costs, these days couture houses also produce prêt-a-porter collections. The purpose of a couture show is to enhance the prestige of the house.

In 1946 there were 106 official haute couture houses. Over the course of the twentieth century, this number dropped dramatically to 18 and today there may be as few as 15, including: Adeline André, Alexandre Vauthier, Alexis Mabille, Chanel, Dior, Franck Sorbier, Givenchy, Jean Paul Gaultier, Schiaparelli and Viktor & Rolf. There are also five correspondent or foreign member houses: Armani, Elie Saab, Versace, Valentino and Giambattista Valli.

# Designing haute couture

The construction of a couture garment may look effortless, but it takes many hours to produce that effortless look. Equipped with a thorough understanding of the human body and knowledge of fibers and fabrics, the couturier may begin with either the fabric or the silhouette.

When the fabric arrives, the couturier drapes unfolded lengths of each fabric over a mannequin or a house model to see how the material hangs on the lengthwise-, cross- and biasgrain lines. Using this information as a guide, he or she starts the design process by drawing sketches for the collection. The design sketches are distributed to the atelier. Depending on the type of garment, the sketches will go to the tailoring workroom (*atelier de tailleur*) or the dressmaking workroom (*atelier de flou*). Then the appropriate weight of muslin/calico is selected and the toile is draped on the mannequins to duplicate the design sketch. This drape provides the basic pattern from which the garment will be sewn.

The toile will be made with all the necessary underpinnings and put together with the same care as the final garment. This toile is then fitted on the house model and reworked. Sometimes toiles are made in the final fabric straight away, allowing the couturier to appreciate the garment to its full potential.

Once the toile is approved, it is carefully taken apart and pressed so that it can serve as a pattern. After the fabric is cut and thread marked, the prototype is ready to be fitted on the house model once again. This process will be repeated until the designer is satisfied. Finally, accessories are selected by the couturier for the press show and the design is entered in the *Livre de fabrication* (production or look-book).

## Haute Couture

Haute couture can be argued as the purest form of artistic fashion with no one garment being replicated twice. The extremely high level of skill that goes into creating these garments is unrivaled with some pieces taking well over 500 hours to make. Houses employ the best and most skilled tailors, seamstresses and artisans to make their creations a reality. Today around 2000 seamstresses are employed in haute couture for an estimated 2000 regular customers worldwide. Prices for day wear start from $9000 (£7000) and can go well into the millions for eveningwear. (Source: http://raconteur.net/culture/paris-the-worlds-fashion-trendsetter)

5.3 Paul Poiret fashion memoir, Francois Baudot, Thames and Hudson (1997). "Batik" full-length evening cloak (1911) and "Chez Poiret" illustration by George Barbier (1912).

## Paul Poiret (1879–1947)

Poiret changed fashion by creating a new silhouette. The cut of his dresses were clean and uncomplicated in contrast to the other dresses worn at the turn of the century. He was inspired by the orient and exoticism. Paul Poiret was also the first to build a virtual fashion empire.

5.4 Balenciaga Paris, Thames and Hudson Ltd (2006). Irving Penn, *Paris Vogue* (1950).

## Balenciaga (1895–1972)

Cristobel Balenciaga's work has a strictly modern appeal. He was a master of the refined, tailored garment that skimmed the body contours. He made the wearer seem taller by pitching the waistline just above the natural waist. He created some of the most powerful styles in the twentieth century and was often called the designers' designer.

## Charles James (1906–1978)

Charles James invented the American haute couture. He created an ideal of female beauty with his magnificent sculptured dresses. James was a perfectionist who combined the science of design with the eroticism of fashion. Influenced by nature, he named his designs after living things such as the "Petal" or the famous "Fourleaf Clover" evening dress.

5.5 Charles James fashion memoir, Richard Martin, Thames and Hudson (1997). The "Balloon" Dress (1955), drawing by Antonio Lopez.

# Tailoring

The term *tailoring* refers not only to specific hand and machine sewing and pressing techniques but also to a garment whose form and contours are not influenced solely by the wearer's body shape. A tailor has the knowledge to keep the structure of a jacket design in place and improve the appearance of the wearer's natural shape. They might, for example, use different materials to underlay and pad the shoulder and chest areas with great precision.

## A history of tailoring

It is generally agreed that the accepted style in menswear in the early nineteenth century has remained recognisably similar

**5.6 E. Tautz AW13.**

to the present day. There has naturally been some re-proportioning of length and silhouette, either more defined or looser, but the components of a tailored suit—the coat, vest and trouser—have a direct line of descent from the end of the Napoleonic wars.

What is most surprising is that the color palette of these early years has remained virtually unchanged. The use of dark, neutrally colored wool juxtaposed with white linen or cotton reflected a new mood in society. A growing awareness of the importance of hygiene made the wearing of fresh linen an obvious demonstration that cleanliness was indeed next to godliness. George "Beau" Brummell, 1778–1840, an early practitioner of this new concept of dress, was fastidious in his cleanliness, discarding several cravats at one dressing as not being suitably washed, pressed and finished. He awakened a more general interest in neat dressing and gave a great example of a well-dressed man himself.

Since the first tailor's establishment opened in 1785, London's Savile Row has become world renowned for custom-tailored suiting (also called "bespoke" tailoring, because cloth reserved for a customer was "spoken for" by him).

In 1969, Tommy Nutter and Edward Sexton opened their shop Nutters. They pioneered shop window display and revolutionised Savile Row. Today, Ozwald Boateng, Richard James and Timothy Everest are among a new wave of master tailors who cater for those requiring a perfectly fitted suit of outstanding quality and craftsmanship.

Tailoring is a time-honored skill that is complex and specialised in its technical knowledge. Many professionals in the fashion industry worship the tailor's craft and would not attempt to undertake tailored apparel. Organized in guilds and brotherhoods, the tailoring trade has been protected by the people working in it, who pass on and safeguard knowledge very carefully.

Over time, new machinery and fusing materials have been introduced to the tailor's market. However, many are not convinced and prefer to use only hand sewing methods to ensure the precise shaping of the fabric. A sewing machine is only used to close up seams and darts.

Today, tailoring can be split into two categories: traditional custom-tailors who continue to practice their craft more or less as it was a century ago, and industrial tailors, who use speedier and therefore less expensive alternatives and construct their jackets and coats to an industrial tailored finish. This means that the chest pieces, pockets, collar and shoulders are reinforced by an iron-on interlining and prefabricated pieces. Pad stitching (pad stitch is used to join two layers of materials together using a diagonal stitch which is staggered from one row to the next) is replaced by a machine stitch that replicates the stitching pattern. The shoulder roll is machine stitched into the sleeve head instead of being hand sewn and can therefore be carefully placed to the individual requirements of the customer. The industrial tailored suit can be manufactured to a very high standard, but it will never deliver the individual fit and exclusive feel of a custom-tailored suit.

**5.7 A tailor at work, Henry Poole & Co.**

# Tailoring techniques

A lot of components play a significant role in creating an excellently fitted tailored garment, from the right choice of fabric and the shape and design of the garments, to the skilled measuring of the body and the specific techniques employed.

This section will introduce you to some of the materials and techniques used by tailors for constructing jackets.

**5.8 An inside-out tailored jacket showing the under structure.**

**5.9 Woollen fabric and lining sample booklet, published by 2000 Tailoring Ltd. London.**

## The understructure

This is made from different kinds of canvas and interfacing, soft cotton flannel, cotton twill tape, strips of cotton or lambswool, melton for the collar stand, pocketing fabric and strong, lightweight lining.

## The fabrics

Woollen fabric used for tailored suits can fall into two categories: worsteds and woollens. Worsted fabric is woven from long, finely combed wool. It is a firm fabric with a flat surface, ideal for traditional tailored business suits. Woollen fabrics are woven from shorter, uncombed wool fibers. These fibers are loosely twisted and woven much less tightly than the worsteds. The effect is a soft, easy fabric, such as a Harris Tweed. Other fabrics can also be used, such as silk and linen.

## Tweed

A woollen fabric named after the river Tweed, which flows through the Scottish Borders textile areas. Harris Tweed is one variation, made from pure virgin wool that is dyed and spun in Harris (in the Outer Hebrides) and hand woven by the islanders in their homes.

## The hand stitches

The following stitches are commonly used in tailoring:

Basting stitch attaches two or more pieces of fabric temporarily. It is also used to make construction and placement lines.

Pad stitching is used to attach the sew-in interfacing and to shape the garment at the same time.

Slip-stitch attaches the lining edge to the hem invisibly as well as the edges of pockets to the garment.

Fell stitching holds the stay tape (a narrow fabric tape) in place.

Cross-stitch invisibly secures interfacing edges to the garment.

Hemstitching invisibly attaches the hem allowance to the garment.

Tailor's tacks are used to mark fabrics, for example, on the folding line of the lapel rolling line or pocket placement.

## Trimming, notching and grading

All edges in a tailored garment should be flat and sharp without noticeable bulk. Seam edges, collar tips and pocket flaps should roll slightly to the inside, towards the body. To avoid bulky seams use the following methods:

**5.10 Tailored jacket with basting stitching in working progress.**

- Trimming. Trim sewn-in interfacings close to the seam lines. The seam allowance of the collar, lapel and bagged-out pocket points can also be trimmed.
- Notching. Notch the seam allowance by taking out wedges at the outside curves. On a deep curve, bring notches closer together than on a shallow one. Always notch close to the stitching line!
- Grading. Trim the seam allowance back in a staggered fashion whereby the widest seam allowance is layered towards the garment's right side. This is done to cushion the remaining seams so they do not show through to the right side.

## The pressing techniques

Darts and seams create shape in a piece of fabric. It is best, therefore, to use a tailor's ham or a rounded pressing board to maintain the shape. Press the vertical darts towards center front or center back. If using a thick fabric, cut open the dart and press flat. To get a nice, flat point at the dart end, use a needle and insert right to the point. Press with the needle in place and remove it afterwards.

To avoid over pressing, which causes the imprint of seams, edges and darts to appear on the outside, use paper strips or pieces of the same kind of fabric to underlay the seam allowance and edges.

Molding is the stretching and shrinking of fabric to fit the body shape. The best fabric to use is wool, which takes on the new shape and holds it as if it had always been that way. A tailor would reshape the two-piece sleeve to accentuate the forward bend in the elbow area. The trouser leg would be reshaped before a seam allowance is attached. For example, the back panel on the inside leg is stretched at the top to fit on to the front panel, thus achieving a closer fit to the bottom and crotch area.

## The taping

On a jacket, certain areas need to be taped with cotton twill tape. This avoids stretching during construction and strengthens the edges to prevent the jacket losing its shape when worn.

The areas to tape are:

- Neckline
- Armhole
- The fold in the lapel
- The edges of the lapel all the way down to the hemline (some tailors continue along the edge of the front hemline)

When taping an edge, take the measurement from the pattern for the tape length. You will find that the fabric edge has already stretched a bit and that you have to ease the fabric on to the tape.

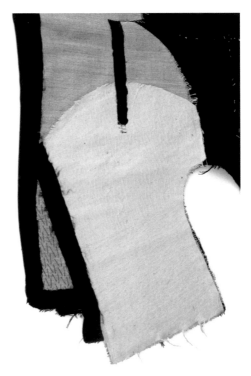

**5.11 Inside the front piece of a jacket showing the taped folding line and taped edges of the lapel.**

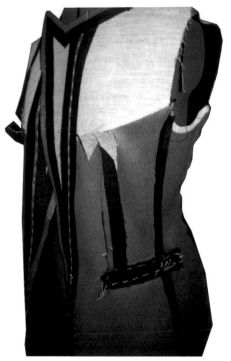

5.12 Example of taping and jacket preparation.

5.13 Walter van Bierendonck SS16.

## The collar and lapel

Collars and lapels can change shape with fashion or can keep a traditional look. The line where collar and lapel meet is called a gorge line.

There are different shapes of lapel used in tailoring:

- Cloverleaf lapel
- Fish mouth lapel
- L-shaped lapel
- Notched lapel
- Peaked lapel
- Shawl collar

## The pocket shapes

The most popular pocket shapes are:

- Welt pocket
- Jetted pocket/piping pocket
- Jetted pocket/piping pocket with flap
- Patch pocket
- Lining/inside pocket

## The fastenings

The placement of buttons is crucial: always place a button half an inch below the natural waistline.

A hand-sewn keyhole buttonhole with inserted gimp is the tailor's choice of fastening on a jacket.

Single-breasted jackets should have one or three buttons; doublebreasted jackets should have four or six buttons, fastened at the second or third.

Sleeve fastenings are traditionally vents, with a button and buttonhole, which sit at the back of the sleeve. The vent can also be opened with a zip or without any fastenings at all.

## Inspired practitioners

### Stuart McMillan, Womenswear Design Director

Stuart is Design Director, Wovens-MMK for Michael Kors where he oversees the structured woven team including Tailoring, Outerwear, Leather, Denim and Fur. He is an experienced design lecturer who has taught at the Royal College of Art, London, UK.

**Where did you train?**
University of Westminster and Royal College of Art.

**What experimentation do you undertake when working with new silhouette shapes?**
A great deal of my time designing is worked directly on the stand or human form. To find new ideas, silhouettes and proportions on the body, I find it successful to work on the form, encouraging a more personal response.

When I drape, I either drape with the fabric I intend to make the garment in or experiment with other fabrics, as this helps define the subtlety between some silhouettes.

**What challenges do you have to overcome when putting a collection together?**
Many. There are many process when designing, whether you design for yourself, a ready-to-wear brand or a high street brand. Initially it's understanding your customer, what your focus or research is for the season, color and fabrics. Having a team of designers is one of the main challenges in order to make sure the line is consistent and the brand's "signature" is maintained while having input from many different designers with their own unique signature.

Other realities quite recently is understanding the global market, as some high-end designers shift from the catwalk schedule to a retail model, the future of how fashion is presented to the customer is evolving. It's an exciting time but also a reality of the fashion industry that the designer, brands and students need to learn to adapt and evolve with modern thinking.

**Which elements of tailoring excite you?**

When talking about bespoke tailoring, particularly on Savile Row in London, it's the precision and how a beautifully tailored jacket can enhance the form. The "architectural" nature of building a tailored garment excites me. The various elements, the bricks and mortar if you like, carefully chosen, considered, molded, manipulated and finally perfectly finished, represent days of work and normally decades of experience.

**What advice would you give to an aspiring designer?**

Research. Find out as much as you can about the industry before you decide to invest in university, college or starting your own label. Many young aspiring designers I've met or taught have been surprised how much work and dedication is involved in being a designer. The industry is tough to work in but at the same time rewarding, creative and full of amazing people.

**How important is understanding the construction process in fashion design?**

Extremely important. As a designer, you are involved in so many different processes through a garment's life— from the initial idea to the fittings, and finally hanging in store. Without a history of considered construction and the developed use of materials, the garments look unconsidered and generally poor.

Understanding of construction is also key to the practical reality that many garments are produced in the Far East and normally to a very restrictive timetable. If the construction techniques and knowledge isn't passed on from the designer to the factories at the initial stage, it's very hard to salvage a garment during this fast turn around.

## Task

### Tailoring exercises

1. Design a simple jacket with consideration to the fastening, collar and lapel shape. Draft and pattern cut this into a simple pattern—remember to cut the facing of the jacket out as this will create the lapel. You might also decide to introduce a side panel for shaping.

Your pieces should include:
- Front body (cut 1 pair); block fuse
- Back body (cut 1 pair if CB seam is present); fuse top back and hem
- Side body (cut 1 pair); fuse underarm and hem
- Top sleeve (cut 1 pair); fuse sleeve head and hem
- Under sleeve (cut 1 pair); fuse hem
- Front facing (cut 1 pair); block fuse
- Top collar (cut 1 only); block fuse
- Under collar (cut in melton/felt, or, 1 pair on bias self fabric)
- Front canvas piece (cut 1 pair in horsehair or similar canvas)

2. Lay this pattern onto pre-steamed wool, and chalk these pieces out, paying attention to the straight of grain and which pieces need block fusing or placement fusing. Cut this out.

To understand methods and techniques of stitching in tailoring you have to practice them first.

Using the pieces you have cut out try these reinforcement and hand-sewing techniques:
- Block fusing or basting sew-in interfacing
- Taping edges of jacket—neckline, armhole, lapel etc.
- Pad stitch a sew-in interfacing or horsehair canvas to the lapel
- Basting the front body canvas to the front jacket
- Cross stitch the canvas picking up on the canvas on one side and the wool on the other side (usually in the seam allowance)

Sew the pieces up when prepared with canvas and interfacing, and check the balance of the jacket. Check the pitch of the sleeves and also hand stitch a shoulder pad and sleeve head roll into the sleeve head.

## Further exercise

Buy an existing second-hand tailored jacket and unpick the lining. Turn the jacket inside out and examine the different techniques used to put the jacket together. Try to practice some of these stitching methods and analyze the jacket for fabric content and detail.

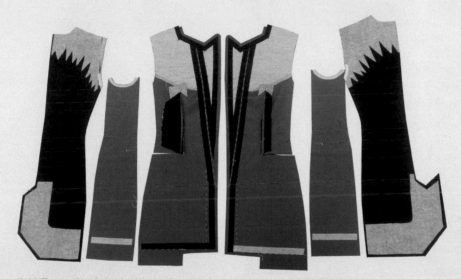

**5.16 Example of the jacket body with fusing, canvas and taping laid flat.**

# Draping on the Mannequin

Draping is modeling or shaping a piece of fabric on a mannequin (also called a model-stand, dress form or dummy) or a life model. Madeleine Vionnet (in the 1920s) and Madame Alix Grès (1930s) were the first couture designers to devote their talent and time to the art of draping. To this day, designers look back on their achievements and recreate their techniques.

For the designer who is looking for a more exciting cut and who is prepared for the unexpected, draping is an excellent way of approaching design and pattern development. Let yourself be inspired by the texture, color and fall of the fabric, and see the design evolve before your eyes.

**6.1 Dior's atelier.**

# Modeling tools and equipment

There is a vast range of mannequins available. It is vital before starting with the drape to have a close look at the model stand you are working on. Take measurements and analyze the general shape of the stand to work out if it covers the look and size you are after. In addition, you should have the following tools and equipment to hand before starting to drape.

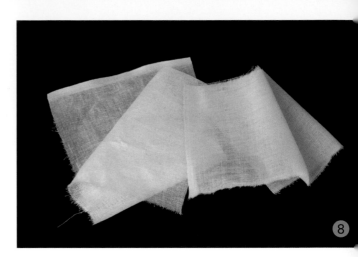

**Marker pen (1)** To mark permanent lines on the garment.

**Scissors and shears (2)** Good quality scissors are important. You will need a small pair of scissors (approximately 8–14 cm) for trimming and notching the fabric and a larger pair of shears (approximately 14–20 cm) to reshape the fabric.

**Tailor's chalk (3)** To mark temporary lines on the garment.

**Camera (4)** It is very useful to have a camera to hand to document all the stages, especially the end result of each drape. To recreate a drape without any points of reference is time consuming and often leads to disappointment.

**Fine pins (5)** Use sharp, fine, non-rusting pins to fix the fabric pieces together and to anchor the fabric to the mannequin.

**Tape measure (6)** Use a 60 in/150 cm tape measure.

**Style tape (7)** Use a narrow (fabric or sticky) tape to mark style lines as well as the bust-, waist- and hiplines.

**Material for draping (8)** The best option is to drape in the final fabric, but this is also the most expensive way. The next best thing is to drape with a material closest in weight, fall and texture to the final fabric. Popular choices are calico, muslin or jersey. These fabrics are inexpensive and the grain line is easy to recognize. Knitwear and jersey garments should always be draped in fabric of a similar character, for example inexpensive knit or jersey.

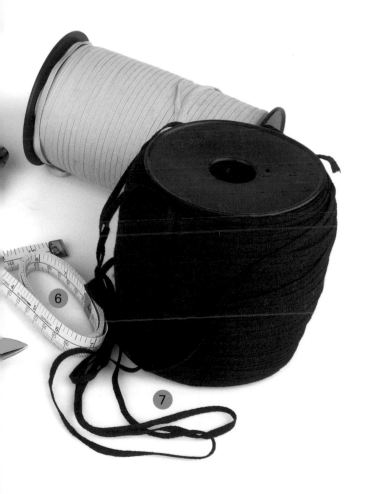

# Grain line and draping

The direction of the grain line will strongly affect how the fabric hangs on the body. The grain line can be used in three different ways.

1. You can start draping the fabric on to the mannequin using the straight grain/lengthwise grain (warp), which runs parallel to the selvedge. This grain line can be used if you want to work close to the body or for garment styles that do not require any stretch.
2. When using the crosswise grain (weft), hold the fabric on to the mannequin so that the selvedge runs parallel to the bust-, waist- or hiplines. The fabric has a little more give/stretch used on the cross than with the straight grain. Fabric on the cross might be used for wider pieces or because of the fabric's pattern/motif or shine.
3. To gain shape without darts and achieve beautiful soft drapes, use a bias grain. Fold one corner of the fabric in a diagonal to the selvedge, creating a 45-degree fold line. This fold line is the true bias.

Experimenting with all three grain lines to start with will give you a good idea about the fall of a fabric. Also take the time to drape different kinds of fabric, such as woven fabrics and jerseys, on to the mannequin and you will instantly see the difference in the draping effect. It is essential to understand the qualities of certain fabrics to be able to use them in the right way and therefore to master the art of draping. A little passion goes a long way.

**6.2 Length grain.**          **6.3 Cross grain.**          **6.4 Bias grain.**

## A balanced pattern

Balancing the pattern of a draped garment ensures that the garment will sit comfortably on the body without swinging to the front, back or either side. Therefore, the side seam of a garment will hang straight up and down and lie correctly on the body. A good way to maintain the balance is by keeping the center front and center back on a perfect grain, using the length grain running from top to bottom and the cross grain aligned with the bust line. To sustain a correct balance between the front and back, make sure that the straight grain and the cross grain are positioned at an angle to the side seam.

Before you take your drape off the mannequin, make sure that you mark all information on to the garment, such as center front and back, side seam position, bustline, waistline, hipline and so on.

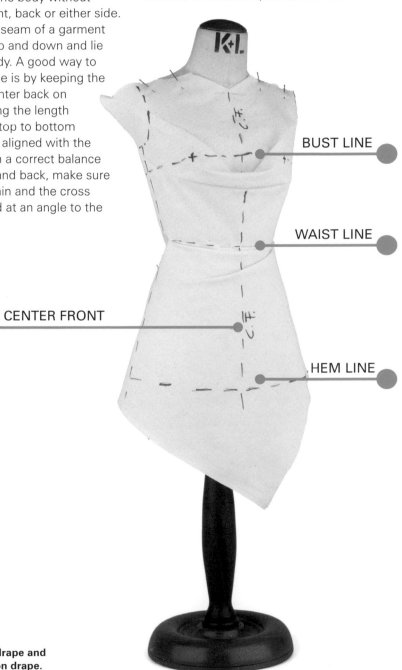

BUST LINE

WAIST LINE

CENTER FRONT

HEM LINE

**6.5 Mannequin with drape and marked information on drape.**

# Draping style

Garments can be draped on to the mannequin, close to the body contour or as an actual shape, structured away from the body. Another approach is loose draping whereby the fabric is anchored on certain parts of the body, such as the shoulder. The fabric hangs loose and drapes fluidly from these points.

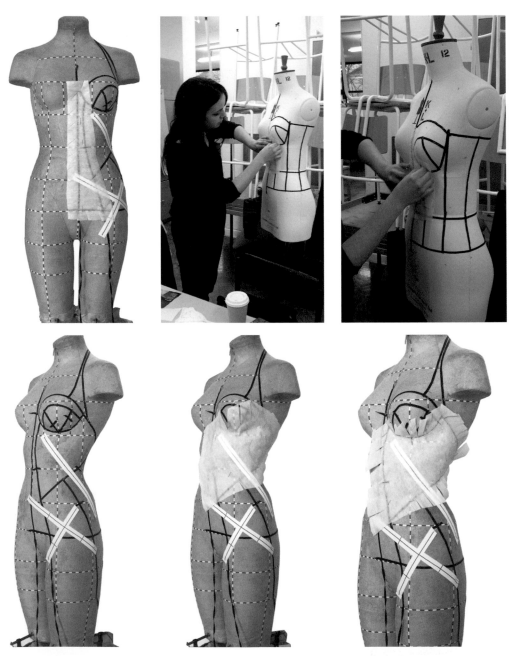

**6.6–6.11 Body contour method developed by Tim Williams, shown on the mannequin.**

## Body contour

During the late 1990s Tim Williams originated lingerie and swimwear for, amongst others, Agent Provocateur and Luella Bartley. He developed a method that enabled him to "draw" the seams and edges on the mannequin and from this, to quickly and accurately create a pattern. Here he explains his body contour technique:

For the body contour method, you are essentially using the dress stand as your basic block. The method very accurately follows the silhouette of the dummy you are using, making contours around the body to enable a close fitting shape that is then created by the seams. I have used this method on body suits for the film industry, lingerie, swimwear and sportswear. I like working this way because you are "drawing" your seams and working in three dimensions from the start.

After you have generated a pattern that fits the stand, you then use pattern manipulation techniques to grade the pattern up and down and increase or decrease any particular parts of the pattern. Remember that creating a pattern to fit a dummy is relatively easy. The next stage, fitting to a person and ensuring comfort and movement, is the most critical application of this technique.

When teaching this method, I always ask the students to make up a sample toile as early as possible from the first pattern so that they can give themselves feedback on how the dummy shape relates to their model's shape.

The equipment needed is primarily your dress stand. If you wish, you can use a shop window stand (symmetrical ones only), but you must first cover it in a tight stretch jersey to enable you to place pins. You will also use a selection of colored biros, some paper, non-woven interfacing and black ¼ in (6 mm) stay tape.

The principle is simple: You mark on the stand where the seams will generate the shape. Like drawing, this simple process relies on the skill of knowing where to place the lines, aesthetically as well as technically.

Always approach this method with a clear idea of what you want in terms of design. Use a swatch of the final fabric so that you can lay it on the surface of the dummy to check how much shaping you need to make. For example, a very rigid fabric with little or no stretch will need a lot of seams or darts to follow the contour of the dummy/body. A stretch jersey, with Lycra for recovery, will form over the body more and so will need fewer seams to allow shape on the garment.

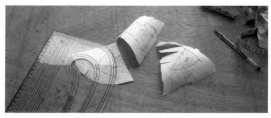

**6.12–6.13 Transferring the pattern to paper.**

**6.14 Lanvin SS16.**

## Loose draping

The other method for draping on the stand is loose draping. Lengths of muslin draped loosely on a mannequin create shapes by the fall of the fabric. Some loose drapes use an understructure, for instance a corset, to which the drape can be attached.

All loosely draped garments need an anchor point, such as the neckline, shoulder, armhole, bust, waist or hip, from which the fabric will drape. It is important to get the grain line just right, as it influences the drape of the fabric.

## Draping tips

- Always use a fabric closest in weight, texture and quality to the final fabric.
- The selvedge is woven more firmly then the rest of the fabric; therefore, snip in to the selvedge to release the tension or cut it off completely.
- Always iron the fabric before starting the drape, as the fabric might shrink.
- Watch the grain line; always use the same grain line you intend to use in the final garment.
- Make sure you use fine pins that slide into the mannequin easily.
- Use a mannequin of the right size and shape.
- Consider shoulder pads or padding out certain parts if necessary before starting the drape.
- Do not be worried about cutting into the fabric—it can be replaced or pinned together if cut too deep.
- Understand what makes a garment look old-fashioned or modern. These days, a more modern look is achieved by, for example, lowering the waist or shortening the shoulder length.
- Always keep in mind the specific style, proportion and detail you are working towards.
- Get the shell right first and then concentrate on the details.
- When draping an asymmetric garment, only drape one side from center front to center back, then later on double the pattern over center front and center back.
- Avoid stretching the fabric onto the mannequin; be light handed.
- Always step away from your work and look at it from a distance or move it in front of a mirror and look at it in reflection.
- Drape for an hour, and if it does not work to your satisfaction step away and approach the drape later after a break.

**6.15 Drape experimentation by Lee Duckworth.**

# Geometric shapes

Using simple geometric shapes can be an exciting way of designing on the mannequin. Cut different sized shapes from circles to squares. They can be draped on their own or stitched together for a different result. Try it out; here are some examples pinned to a mannequin.

**Books to explore**

The art of drape is an exciting one, where unexpected outcomes can occur. Some designers like to start their ideas straight on the stand and build upon that. It can be said that the outcomes of draping are hard to replicate when pattern cutting metrically or flat. The Bibliography lists books for you to explore in drape and shape creation.

**6.16 A skirt constructed from a square.**

**6.17 Circle pattern with armholes.**

**6.18 Triangle and rectangle pattern cut on the bias.**

**6.19 A pattern of two triangles and one strip of rectangle cut on the bias.**

## Inspired practitioners

### Rob Curry, Associate Director of Fashion—3D Design, at the Academy of Art University, San Francisco

Rob is Associate Director of 3D Design, Construction, Draping and Flat Pattern at the Academy of Art University, San Francisco. An experienced academic, pattern cutter and designer, he has worked with Vivienne Westwood as a dressmaker in the Couture Atelier and has collaborated on multiple collections with designers Tristan Webber and Julien Macdonald and worked with Japanese label Unobilie.

**Where did you train?**

I did my degree at Leeds University, then (rather than pursuing further education on an MA course) I did an apprenticeship for two years with Bruce Oldfield, at his Beauchamp Place atelier. I wanted to learn couture skills—train to become a fully rounded dressmaker. An MA was not going to do that.

Being a 3D-inclined person, an apprenticeship was the more beneficial track for me. I needed to work directly with the fabric, learn about the insides of garments and all the hand skills associated with bespoke work. It was there that I really started to learn my craft.

**What is your approach to three-dimensional design?**

It's essential to identify one's motivation for design. What are one's primary concerns when designing? For me, they are concerns of proportion, silhouette, fit, the hang of the fabric and the graphic illusion of seam placements.

As dressmakers, our greatest teacher is Madeleine Vionnet. Beginning my journey in dressmaking, hers was the voice that I heard in my head … questioning … making suggestions. She was a maverick in so many ways. It was from her that I learnt to forget concerns of Fashion and address only concerns of Design.

At the end of the day, a garment is either well made or badly made, well draped or badly draped, well cut or badly cut. Tastes and opinions of aesthetic are subjective. Craftsmanship is not.

**How important is stand work in what you do?**

It is everything. Often I will come up with (what I think at the time as) exciting ideas of how to pattern cut something anew. As an idea it excites and seems to bring a new concept of cut to a project. In three-dimensional form, however, it can possibly fall short. What you must be aware of is that the realization in fabric must work both aesthetically and practically on the body. It is only by working directly on the stand that we can truly observe and analyze the relationship of fabric to form.

## How much of your work is left to chance? Do you enjoy unexpected outcomes?

Unexpected outcomes, or "happy accidents" can be a revelation. They can breathe new life into a project and take you down new paths of experimentation. I wouldn't say that such things are "chance" however. More that, by working the fabric (by cutting and pinning), allowing it to fall and move around the body, new suggestions of proportion, silhouette variations are presented. It is up to us to analyze and react to these suggestions as the fabric dictates. The process must be Observe, Analyze, Comprehend and React.

## Draping vs flat cutting—your thoughts?

There is no issue of one versus the other. Both are part of the process of creation. Whether we chose to begin with one process and follow with the other is dictated by the project itself. By analyzing the concerns of the project, we can proceed as logic dictates. In general, I tend toward more time spent developing a look through draping, especially when the look is a large-scale gown, for example. However, if I'm working with ideas of geometric cut (say, in jersey), then I will initially spend more time with the paper and a ruler, and then move to the stand … then back to the table again. Each informs the other. There is no "either/or" debate.

## How important is balancing traditional and new techniques?

Advances in techniques and technology should enhance and add to our "arsenal" of skills. Just as language evolves to reflect the times we live in, so techniques and technologies evolve, and are developed. But we should not use them to replace the foundation skills, developed over centuries. We can only be truly subversive and forward thinking if we understand and master what came before us. That which is new should not be a crutch to forego learning these foundation skills, but an addition to those skills.

## What advice would you give to an aspiring designer?

It's essential to have a strong sense of self. Who are you, as a designer? What are your personal motivations? Identify your strengths and natural affinities, and make sure your journey doesn't detour via the banal or get sidetracked by superficial concerns.

Whatever area, or specialization you are drawn to, just do it well. Every area of fashion and garment type has its own specific language. Learn that language until you're fluent in it, then you're in a position to subvert it.

It's like being a musician—you have to learn the notes first, in order to forget them, so you can get to the heart of the music.

## Task
### Draping exercises

### Exercise 1
- Drape a closely fitted bodice using a dress stand, with varying style lines. Use tape to mark these style lines on the stand and pin and apply your fabric to this.
- Transfer this drape to paper pattern pieces.
- Cut out in toiling fabric and remake. Check for fit against your original drape.

### Exercise 2
- Drape a bias cut dress or top. Remember to use the grain line on the true 45-degree fold line.
- Transfer this drape to paper pattern pieces.
- Cut out in toiling fabric and remake.

### Exercise 3
- Cut out the following geometric shapes, giving yourself a large piece to start with: square, circle, triangle.

- Use these following shapes to drape three new ideas straight onto the mannequin. Remember, you can use the bias of the fabric or, for a different feel, cut out the shapes in jersey.
- Transfer these drapes to paper pattern.
- Cut out in toiling fabric and remake.

### Further exercises
- Find a picture of a catwalk or designer's dress that has an interesting drape. Make a deduction of what fabric the garment might be and get a similar weight fabric.
- Give yourself three hours and start to drape what you see in the picture being careful of proportion, fullness and balance.
- Transfer this drape to paper pattern pieces and remake.

**6.20 Example of experimental drape.**

# Garment Support and Structure

This chapter offers a brief overview of the history of structured garments and introduces you to the materials and techniques that can be used to achieve support.

Naturally, a fabric will always hang downwards and, depending on the weight, thickness, sheerness, drape and stretch, will align to the body shape. In order to obtain a certain structured look it is necessary to provide support through other materials and techniques. Over the years many designers have complemented or deformed the body shape with the use of clever cutting and structured foundations.

To get the right structure under a garment is one of the most challenging, but most enjoyable, aspects of garment construction. It is important to look into the historical development of dress underpinnings and tailored foundations. There is a lot to learn from the old masters, and it is up to the creative people of today to use their legacy to help create today's and tomorrow's fashions.

**7.1 Long line corset and bra.**

# History of supported and structured garments

Throughout history, dressmakers and tailors have been working hard to achieve a certain body shape in fashion. Since humans first began to cover their bodies, supportive and structured garments have been used and modified. At first, these garments would have been purely for shelter and protection. As time went on, however, clothing began to be associated with social and/or economic status and the interest in structured garments that would accentuate certain parts of the body grew.

By 1860, Britain was approaching the peak of its prosperity as the most highly industrialised nation of the world, and between the 1860s and the 1880s the Victorian woman's dress was at its most complex. Dresses were supported with increasingly heavy boned corsetry, two or three petticoats, hoops and a bustle.

The crinoline (a stiff petticoat or skirt structure) was out of fashion by 1865 and replaced by a more substantial bustle. This was solidly built from horse hair, steel bones and calico.

The social roles of men and women were distinct, and the nineteenth-century female was constrained in her lifestyle choices—she was a dutiful wife or daughter. She was assumed to be weak, fragile and light-headed, something that was not difficult to achieve, as the heavy boned corset would physically weaken women. It was considered bad taste for women not to wear a corset and therefore they would persist in wearing tightly laced corsets, sometimes to such an extent that they could not breathe properly.

By the end of the nineteenth century fashion changed and simple lines began to be regarded as more beautiful. Women still wore tight corsets, but the heavy draped bustle was abandoned.

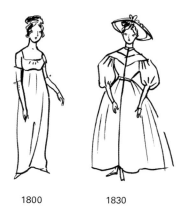

1800          1830

1855          1870

1895

1900-9

Edwardian women were characterised by an S-bend figure and a large bosom. A corset had to be worn as the Edwardians valued a full "hourglass" figure.

The Edwardian silhouette was soon questioned by Paul Poiret, the first designer to build a fashion empire. He replaced the strong boned corset with a softer version and created flowing forms that utilised the "empire" line.

It is a myth of fashion history that women abandoned their corsets during the 1920s. Women wore cylindrical elastic corsets to fit the new silhouettes in fashion, to provide an unbroken line down the whole upper body.

The next major change was heavily influenced by Hollywood and the film industry. In the 1930s, the bosom was back in fashion and women preferred softly sculptural clothes with accentuated feminine contours. This new shape was achieved by wearing shaped brassieres.

In the mid-1930s, corseted crinolines and evening gowns with modified bustles were reintroduced. Royal dressmaker Norman Hartnell was a key figure in this neo-Victorian movement.

1920          New Look

In 1947, at the end of the Second World War, Christian Dior launched his first and now legendary spring collection immortalised as the New Look. In fact, the look was far from new as it revisited the tiny waist and whole circle skirts of the nineteenth century. At the time, everyone wanted to forget about the wartime styles that had been heavily influenced by the rationing of materials. The idea of extravagant amounts of fabric, long full skirts and cinching in women's waists seemed very new and appealing.

To achieve Dior's post-war New Look, corseted underwear to tighten the waist and specially created pads for the hips were used as a foundation to emphasise a strong feminine shape.

As much as the 1950s were elegant and feminine, the 60s were characterised by a cool style influenced by the music of the era. Fashion became youthful: bright colors, pop art, space age influences and synthetic fabrics were all "in."

By the liberated 1970s, corseted bras and underskirts were used only for special occasions and eveningwear and this is still the case today. Corsets are no longer considered necessary and women prefer to shape their bodies by means of diet and exercise.

1911          1912-13

# Supporting materials

The range of available supporting materials is vast. These days, we still use the well-established technique of boning to support corsetry and underskirts. Creating thickness and bulk can also be achieved using wadding as an added layer to fabric.

You will find different weights of netting under a garment for bulk or lift. Padding can also be used to create shape and volume and to emphasise parts of the body. Padding can give more definition and form to a garment; quilted fabric will look crisp and stiff, standing away from the body and wadding can be used to create structure and insulation.

Interfacing/interlining is primarily used to support and add substance to fabric. It comes in two versions: fusible (iron-on) and non-fusible (sewn-in). On a traditional shirt, the collar, cuffs and button-fly would not be without its use. Canvas is also used as interfacing on parts of a garment that require more body; for example, the front of a tailored jacket.

Fabrics such as organza, organdie and cotton muslin all work very well as backings for other fabrics that require body and stability.

Crinoline and rigid interlining stiffen and add solid support to sculpted garments.

It is interesting to research upholstery and curtain making to get some ideas of different materials and techniques. Books on equestrian wear, shoe or bag making also have lots of great ideas for inspiration when designing supported and structured garments.

1. Canvas
2. Fusible and non-fusible tape
3. Iron-on interlining/fusing
4. Rigid interlining for extreme support
5. Tailor's front supporting piece with canvas and wadding
6. Tailored shoulder pads
7. Shoulder roll
8. Crinoline
9. Boning, plastic and metal with plastic coating
10. Wadding
11. Raglan shoulder pads

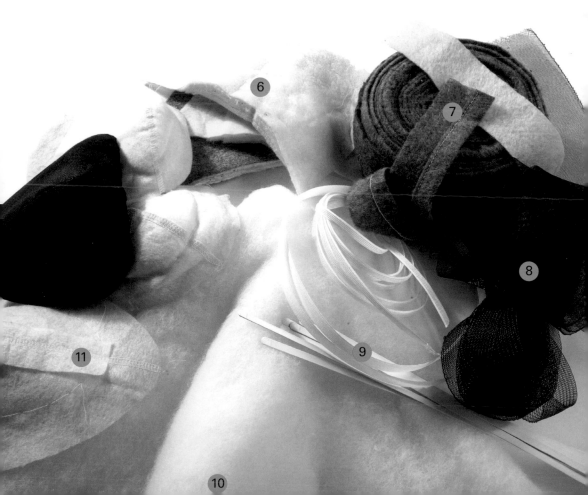

## Netting

Net is an open-mesh, transparent fabric. It is one of the oldest fabrics known, available in a variety of natural and man-made fibers, such as silk, cotton, rayon, polyester and nylon. It can range from very sheer to stiff and heavy. The finer version of netting is called tulle and shows a hexagonal pattern.

Netting is mainly used as a supporting material. It can be made into a petticoat or underskirt by gathering the netting into one or more layers of multi-tiered net. The amount used depends on the volume required. Netting can be used as an interfacing and underlining, as it adds crispness without weight. It is also suitable as a base for lace appliqués. Net is not only used for the inside of garments—some variations give great effects when used for the final garment, too.

Net has no grain line and has more give in the width than in the length. Remember this when cutting the fabric in order to get the best use out of it. Care must be taken when working with net, as it has a tendency to rip easily. It does not fray, but a raw edge may irritate the wearer's skin. To prevent this, it can be finished with a binding or a lace or net facing.

### Netting varieties

Illusion is one of the finest nets and is often used as decoration on garments such as bridal veils.

Maline is a fine netting with hexagonal patterned holes. It is used mainly for millinery.

Point d'esprit is a fine net with dots on a repeated interval; it is mostly used for decoration.

Tulle is also a fine netting and can be used as is or it can be starched—such as for ballet tutus.

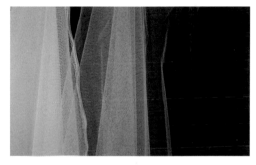

**7.3 Different types of netting.**

**7.4 Christian Dior skirt with netting inlay attached for more volume.**

**7.2 Marchesa SS16.**

## Quilting

Quilted fabrics are available in two-layered and three-layered versions. The two-layered version has a top or face layer made of decorative fabric. The second layer is wadding, which is made out of cotton or synthetic fiber batting. Traditionally, both layers are stitched together in a series of seam diagonals to form a diamond pattern. Two-layered quilting is mostly used for lining to insulate a garment.

A three-layered quilted fabric can be single-faced or double-faced. When single-faced, the top or face layer is usually a decorative fabric over a lightweight tricot, lining or gauze backing. In between is a layer of wadding, and all three layers are machine quilted together.

The double-faced quilted fabric has two top or face layers and a layer of wadding sandwiched in between, all of which are machine quilted together.

Some quilting fabrics are thicker than others, depending on the separate layers and thickness of wadding. A quilted material appears stiff and crisp and stands away from the body. Some designers create their own quilted fabrics and stitching technique for a unique, decorative effect.

Quilt is also used as a means of protection, such as on motorcycling gear and other sports garments.

**7.5 J.W Anderson AW16.**

## Padding

Padding a garment helps to emphasise parts of the body, to add shape and support or it can simply make a fashion statement. Padding involves creating a tunnel or shape, which then can be stuffed with lambswool, polyester fleece, cotton batting or armo wool. One early example of an exceptional use of padding is an evening dress by Elsa Schiaparelli (1890–1973), a designer with a strong interest in surrealism. The dress is a black skeleton evening gown with a padded representation of human bones.

Christian Dior also created exceptional padded designs with his New Look collection. Here, he created pads to emphasise the hip for a stronger feminine look. Modern designers Victor & Rolf showed an experimental way of using padded sculptured pieces with garments draped on top in their 1998/1999 Autumn/Winter collection. The beauty of the concept was that all the clothes could be worn with or without the padded pieces.

Padding can also be used in hemlines, to soften and add weight and body to a hem. The advantage of a well-padded hem is that it provides protection from overpressing and keeps its softness for the lifetime of the garment.

**7.6 BAR lady's suit by Christian Dior from the New Look collection.**

## Shoulder pads

A shoulder pad is used to define the shoulder area and create a smooth appearance over the shoulder and collarbone. Pads are used between the garment fabric and the lining, or covered pads can be used inside the garment on the shoulder.

Shoulder pads come in different sizes and shapes. Depending on the sleeve design, there are several shapes available. For example, the tailored pad is triangular and made from layers of wadding sandwiched between felt, which is then loosely stitched together. The tailored pads used in women's and men's jackets or coats are approximately $3/8$–$9/16$ in (1–1.5 cm) high over the shoulder point. The height can be customised and layers can be added to accommodate a different look.

Pads are also available for raglan sleeves—a raglan sleeve has a much softer appearance and therefore the pad is an oval shape. The tailored pad used in a set-in sleeve is cut off at the end of the shoulder to create a strong and square appearance, whereas the raglan shoulder pad runs along the shoulder and into the sleeve for a softer look.

Regular pads can be bought readymade in haberdashery shops or, for a better result, can be created from scratch using the pattern of the garment so that the fit and form are perfect. Designers have to consider the extra costs when using a bespoke shoulder pad, but such costs are likely to be counterbalanced by the creation of a better, perhaps more exciting silhouette.

During the 1980s and early 1990s, shoulder pads were especially popular with fashion designers. Garments such as blouses and jersey pieces were available with detachable pads. Growing up in the 1980s, women would fill their accessory drawers with different sizes and shapes of shoulder pads that could then be added under all kinds of outfits.

### Feminine tailoring

At the beginning of the 1980s, a new clothing style was b.orn. Famous women in US television programs, such as *Dallas* and *Dynasty*, as well as influential women in politics and business made this style successful. It soon became popularly known as "power dressing." This is instantly recognizable by the use of expensive materials such as silk and a powerful, masculine cut. Both men and women wore suits, and the style was intended to convey an impression of competence and authority.

**7.7 A tailored shoulder pad (left) and a raglan shoulder pad (right).**

**7.8 Raglan and tailored shoulder pads in different shapes and sizes.**

# Interlining/Fusing

Interlining/fusing is used at certain
parts of the garments to add body and
stability. It is available as fusible interlining
(adhesive dots that melt when ironed on
to the fabric), or in a non-fusible form for
sewing in. You will find more information
about interlining and fusing on p. 154.

## Where to use interlining and fusing

Some parts of a garment need
reinforcement. Critical points, such as
buttonholes and buttons, for example,
must be strengthened to enable them
to withstand high levels of pulling. Areas
such as the waistband on a skirt or trouser
also need to be tough in order to stand up
to all the movement experienced around
this area. Collars and cuffs, which are
expected to stand up and look the same
after several launderings, will also need to
be reinforced.

Reinforce the following areas by fusing:

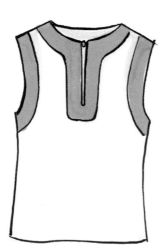

### Facings

- Facing. Fuse completely the facing
around the neckline and armhole.

### The shirt

- Shirt collar. Fuse under-collar, topcollar
and collar stand.
- Button stand.
- Fuse complete button stand.
- Cuffs. Fuse complete cuff and cuff fly
opening.

### The trouser

- Waistband. Fuse the complete
waistband.
- Belt loops. Fuse the complete belt
loops.
- Pocket. Fuse the pocket mouth with a
$^{13}/_{16}$–$^{13}/_{16}$ in (2–3 cm) stripe of fusing.
- Zip fly. Fuse under wrap and over wrap
of the zip fly.

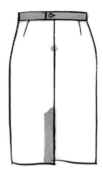

### The jacket

- Front. Fuse the complete front with a fusible interfacing.
- Collar. Fuse the collar and lapel with a stitch-reinforced fusing.
- Front facing. Fuse completely with a stitch-reinforced fusing.
- Pocket. Fuse the pocket mouth using a $^{13}/_{16}$–$1^3/_{16}$ in (2–3 cm) strip of stitch-reinforced fusing, and interface the jets for the jetted pocket.
- Back. Fuse the top of the back panels.
- Sleeve. Fuse the top of the sleeve head and the button fly and hem facing.
- Hem. Fuse the hem facing completely and $^3/_8$ in (1 cm) past the breakline.
- Vent. Fuse the complete under wrap of the vent and the facing of the over wrap

### The skirt

- Waistband. Fuse the complete waistband.
- Pocket. Fuse the pocket mouth and the jets for the jetted pocket.

- Zip. Cut out a small circular shape of fusing and reinforce the zip end.
- Vent. Fuse the complete under wrap of the vent and the facing of the over wrap.

### Belts

- Belt. Reinforce the complete belt.

### Working with interlining

When cutting out the interlining, make sure to cut the pieces $^3/_{16}$ in (5 mm) smaller around the edges than the pattern piece itself. This is to avoid the interfacing hanging over the fabric edges and therefore sticking on to the iron table or fusing machine. It is also important to avoid a heavy edging whereby the fusing runs right up to the edge. It is much better to work in layers.

## Fusible interlining

There are three steps to note when using a fusible (iron-on) interlining.

### Heat

The heat of the iron or fusing machine has to be compatible with the adhesive used on the interlining and the fabric.

### Pressure

The fusing may not become attached to the fabric if the pressure is too low.

### Time

Depending on the melting point of the adhesive and the pressure applied to the lining and fabric, the time has to be set right. If too little time is allowed, the adhesive might not melt to the fabric.

Fusible interlinings are available in a variety of types to suit all kinds of fabrics. Some have adhesive dots close together for more body cover and less movement in the fabric, which adds stability. Some have adhesive dots further apart, which creates softer and more lightweight fusing in order to allow more flexibility in the fabric.

Thread reinforced interlining is also available in two versions. The first is horizontally and vertically reinforced interlining, which contains vertical threads for a high level of stability and horizontal threads for additional flexibility. The other kind of interlining contains only vertical threads, creating vertical stability. Both versions have a grain line following the thread so this must be considered when cutting out.

A range of specialized interlinings is also available. For example, leather and fur are sensitive to heat and should therefore be fused with an interlining that has an adhesive with a low melting point. Stretch fabrics, jersey and knitwear can be stabilized in every direction with a jersey fusing. Jersey fusing is also suitable for interlining loose-woven fabrics in order to retain the softness and movement of the fabric.

**7.9 Different samples of fusible interlining.**

## Non-fusible interlining

Non-fusible, sewn-in interlining achieves similar effects to the fusible variety. For a better result, some fabrics should be underlaid with materials such as muslin, organza, organdie or crinoline. For example, a full skirt on an evening gown made from silk duchess would benefit from an underlayer of silk organza, which adds support and permanent shape to the garment. Similarly, the use of an open-weave woollen or cotton fabric between the lining and outer fabric in a winter coat would create extra warmth.

Classic shirts make extensive use of interlining to support the collar, cuffs and button stand. On a trouser or skirt, the waistband, facing, pocket mouth, zip-fly and sometimes the hem are often interlined. The collar, lapel, facing, pocket mouth, fastening, vent and hemline of a jacket or coat would also be supported in this way.

**7.10 Different samples of nonfusible interlining.**

**7.11–7.12 Examples of a jacket that has been fused to add support and body to the fabric and shape of the jacket.**

## Canvas interfacing

Canvas is another type of interfacing, which can be set between the lining, facing and outer fabric. It is used where the garment requires more body and long-lasting shape. Canvas is a combination of hair and wool threads with horsehair twists or viscose filaments. For supporting the pockets, the use of a linen canvas or linen/hair canvas is advisable. It will support the pocket mouth so that it stays permanently in shape.

Canvas is also used as interfacing in traditional jackets and coats to support the shape of the jacket (rather than the shape of the person wearing it). The purpose of the canvas is to control the fabric and reduce its tendency to wrinkle and stretch.

Canvas was, and still is, used in corsets and underskirts.

**7.14 Canvas samples.**

**7.13 Jacket inside, canvas as chest piece and shoulder support.**

**7.15 Pre-finished canvas piece.**

# Corsetry

A corset is a close-fitting bodice, stiffened with boning. The role of the corset is to shape the body and to impose a fashionable silhouette upon it. The word was used during the seventeenth and eighteenth centuries but became more common in the nineteenth century, replacing the word "corps." Over time, corsetry would be used to control and shape three main areas of a body: the bust, waist and hips. Corsetry often worked against nature and therefore created an illusion.

7.16–7.17 1940s/50s bras with waist support.

7.18 1930s girdle with support for waist to hip by elastic fabric.

## Boning

Boning was originally made from whalebone in constructed undergarments such as corsetry. Today we have a choice of two materials: metal or plastic. Rigilene ® is a particular type of plastic boning made from fine polyester rods.

Metal boning needs a casing or tunnel prepared; the bone slides into it and is therefore covered up. Plastic boning can be stitched onto the foundation and only needs covering up on the cutting-off lines.

Depending on the style of corset, boning can be placed from the hip to the waist, and into and around the bust. The boning can be stitched on to the wrong side of the outer fabric as a design effect or worked into the foundation of the corset.

**7.19 A selection of traditional and modern boning materials:
Rigilene (a)
Metal (b)
Plastic (c)**

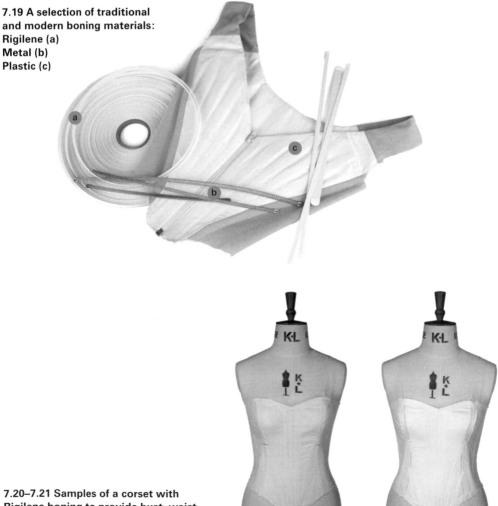

**7.20–7.21 Samples of a corset with Rigilene boning to provide bust, waist and abdomen support.**

## Materials for constructing a corset

Cotton drill and coutil are strong natural materials with flexibility. The twill weave is one of the stronger weave techniques and fabric made in this way is therefore suitable for a foundation of a corset. It provides the base for applying the boning.

Mesh is a stretch powernet made of synthetic fiber, used to give more flexibility.

Canvas is a substantial material made from a combination of hair and wool threads with horsehair twists or viscose filaments. It is used in corsetry to control the fabric and reduce its tendency to wrinkle and stretch.

Interlining/fusing is a woven or nonwoven fabric that can be ironed on or sewn in to support and add substance to any fabric used for the foundation of a corset.

Brushed cotton is a light cotton fabric that is brushed on one side of the fabric to achieve a soft and cushioned effect. It is placed between the boned foundation of the corset and the outer fabric to prevent the boning from showing through.

Supporting materials are used when the natural body of the outer fabric is not strong enough. Fabrics such as muslin, organza and organdie are used for support. The supporting materials would be mounted (mounting stitches are medium hand stitches around the edge of the fabric piece) and the two fabrics used as one.

Lining is a very thin fabric made of silk, viscose or synthetic fibers. Its purpose is to protect the skin from the boned foundation and to clean up the inside of the corset for a good quality finish.

Laces, hook-and-eye fastenings and zips can all be used to fasten corsetry.

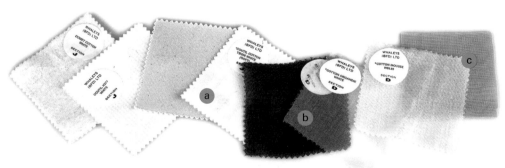

**7.22 A selection of materials for constructing a corset:**
**Cotton drill (a)**
**Organza (b)**
**Mesh powernet (c)**

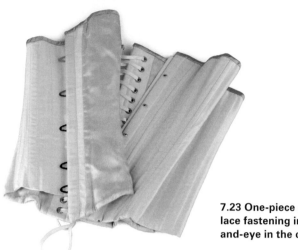

**7.23 One-piece strapless corset with lace fastening in the back and hook-and-eye in the center front.**

**7.24 Corselet foundation with boning, powernet and inner belt, fasten by hook-and-eye underneath the zip and garters.**

**7.25 The inside of a black velvet corset by Vivienne Westwood, with boning in the center front and center back, powernet as side panels and straps and a zip fastening.**

# Creating volume

Adding volume to a garment means changing the dimensions to create a larger silhouette. This can be done by adding volume through seams and darts or gathers, pleats and drapes, as well as by adding flare. The right fabrics can also help to increase the volume on a garment.

## Volume through drapes

Draping techniques can be used to achieve a soft look with added volume. A drape is excess fabric falling down (draping) from one anchor point or between two or more anchor points. The cowl drape is one of the more controlled drapes and works well on tops, sleeves or skirts. Irregular and uncontrolled drapes can also be created. These are done on the mannequin and not as a flat pattern construction.

## Volume through flare

A flared garment is fitted at one point, such as the waist, and gradually widens to the other end of the garment, such as the hemline of a skirt. Flare in a garment is usually loose swinging and not controlled through pleats or gathers. The method used to add flare to a garment can be slash and spread or by simply adding on flare to

the seams, such as the side seam, and ignoring darts such as the waist dart.

## Volume through fabric

Using the right fabric for a garment that has been designed to come off the body shape is important. If the garment achieves more volume through drapes, gathers or pleats, more fabric needs to be provided. On the other hand, if volume is added by cut and construction, such as for a sculptured piece, the right weight, texture and density of the fabric is essential.

**7.26 Marques'Almeida SS16.**

## Creating volume with godets

Seams and darts are not only used for shaping a garment to the body but also for expanding shape away from the body. Seams can be used to add in extra pieces of fabric for more volume, such as godets.

A godet is traditionally a triangular-shaped piece of fabric set into a seam or a cut line. Godets are used to add extra fullness as much as being a design feature. The shape of a godet varies—it can be pointed, round or even squared on the top and constructed as a half-, three-quarter- or full-circle.

The most common use of godets is in skirts, but they can also be added into sleeves, trouser bottoms, bodices and so on.

When stitching in a pointed godet, extra care needs to be taken with the top point. Seam allowance can be limited and the top point can tear easily and fray. It is therefore advisable to strengthen the top point with interlining before sewing in the godet. To achieve a pointed top, first stitch one side of the godet from the hemline to the top point and secure, then take it out of the sewing machine and start again on the other side, from hemline to the top point. Try this first on a sample piece of fabric before attempting to sew the final garment.

**7.27 Circle-shaped godet.**

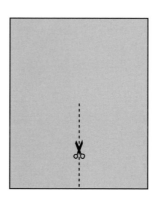

**7.28 Cutting line on garment.**

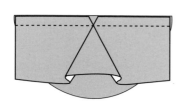

**7.29 Straighten out the cutting line to insert the godet.**

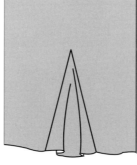

**7.30 Good side of the garment.**

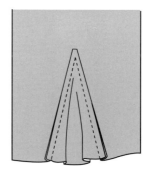

**7.31 Wrong side of the garment.**

## Creating volume with gore panels

The gore skirt has a similar look to the godet skirt except that there are no inserts. The skirt is wide at the hem and shaped to the waist. A gore skirt can start with four gores, which have seams at the sides, center front and center back, and there can be as many as 24 gores in a skirt. Depending on the look, the gores are equally spaced or random. The skirt may hang straight from the hip or any point below, be flared or pleated or have an uneven hemline.

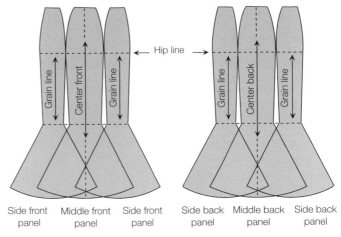

Side front
panel | Middle front
panel | Side front
panel | Side back
panel | Middle back
panel | Side back
panel

**7.32 Pattern pieces for a six-piece gore skirt.**

**7.33 Marchesa SS16.**

## Creating volume through gathers and pleats

Applying gathers is a great way of creating volume.

- Take the fabric edge that is meant to be gathered and place under the sewing machine. Turn the stitch length to the largest stitch ($^3/_{16}$ in [4–5 mm]).
- Start sewing about $^3/_{16}$–$^1/_4$ in (5–7 mm) away from the fabric edge. Sew from the start to the finish of the gathering line. Sew a second line a couple of millimeters below the first.
- Take the top threads from both sewing lines and pull.
- As you pull the thread, the fabric will bunch up and create gathers, which can be equally spaced or irregular depending on the design.

Pleats, like gathers, will create instant volume. A pleat is folded fabric, held down securely along joining seam lines. It can be pressed down or left soft. The volume created by pleats depends on the number of pleats and the pleat depth.

**7.34 Pleating experimentation by Charlotte Roden.**

**7.35 Toile line up and detail of pleating by Charlotte Roden.**

**7.36 Comme Des Garcons AW16.**

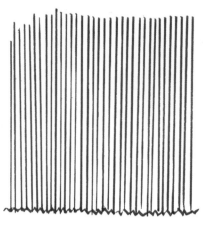

**7.38 Crystal pleats.**

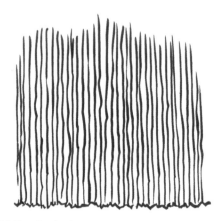

**7.37 Dress by Puccini with sunray pleated detail under the arm.**

**7.39 Tree bark pleats.**

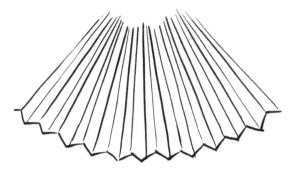

**7.40 Sunray pleats.**

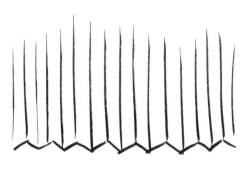

**7.41 Box pleats.**

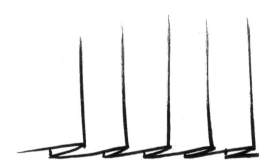

**7.42 Plain knife pleats.**

**7.43 Accordian pleats.**

## Inspired practitioners

### Rosie Armstrong, Lecturer & Pattern Cutter

Rosie is a Senior Lecturer at the University of Westminster, London, UK and is an experienced pattern cutter, working for select industry clients on a freelance basis. Rosie previously worked as Senior Menswear Technician at the Royal College of Art, London, UK and has over 13 years' experience in the fashion industry, which includes creating showpieces for Alexander McQueen and designing for Tommy Hilfiger and Topman.

**Where did you train?**

I gained a first class BA (Hons) in Fashion Design with Knitwear at Central Saint Martins and an MA in Fashion Knitwear Design at the Royal College of Art. Whilst I was studying at Central Saint Martins, I undertook a placement at Alexander McQueen, which led to a job as Womenswear Creative Cutter working mainly on producing the complex show-pieces from pattern through to garment. Alongside this, I was taking a traditional tailoring course in the costume department at the Royal Exchange Theatre in Manchester and also in the knitwear department at Missoni. After the RCA, I worked at Tommy Hilfiger in Amsterdam where I gained experience with large-scale production and communicating with producers to ensure the final garments were as I envisioned. The range of experience from my training has been invaluable to offering my students a wide variety of approaches to design realization.

**Can you explain your role?**

For six years, I worked at the Royal College of Art as the Senior Menswear Technician. In this role, I worked with the students to help them realize their designs in 3D. Through technical workshops, fittings and one-to-one support, I trained them to pattern cut and construct garments and advised them on the approach to best create their desired fit, silhouette and the overall appearance of the finished pieces. My driving force was to enable the students and to give them the skills and tools to independently analyze their designs, produce their patterns and both the ability to make their own garments or direct someone else to produce them.

I currently work freelance as an Associate Lecturer in Fashion at Westminster University and as a pattern cutter and seamstress for a wide range of private clients and fashion houses.

## How would you approach using experimental fabrics?

Testing and sampling is really important when using experimental fabrics. I would buy a reasonable sized piece and work with it on traditional sewing machines to test if they can be used or if new techniques and machinery need to be used. Crucially, I would test to see if the fabric can be washed or ironed and if water, heat or steam changes its appearance or characteristic. I would create sample seams and details from my design trying different approaches to understand what works best. Making large test samples would enable me to see if the fabric is likely to change the way a garment fits; for example, if it is stiff or bulky, or the hang of the garment is drapey or lacks flexibility. I would also ask people who have experience of working with the fabric and glean anything I can from them. I am still and will always be learning.

## Could you explain your ideas on correct fitting?

I am not sure that there is a "correct fit" as such. Having said that, some things are essential, like the wearer being able to lift their arms, getting into and out of the garment and movement, and there needs to be enough space in the crotch. Trends in fit have changed so much over time and will continue to change. I suppose I would say that correct fit is creating real garments that are 3D realizations of the original 2D design.

## What challenges do you see students face when trying to realize their designs? How can they overcome them?

I think it can be daunting for students to know where to start. Every design requires a different approach, and it can be difficult to know the best approach to take in any given situation. To begin with, it can be hard to know which block to use and whether to flat pattern cut or drape on the stand. Fitting on a model is essential, as people are a different shape to the mannequins, and how they move has an affect on how the garment should fit. During fitting, changes to fit and silhouette can change the balance, tension and hang of the garment and students can find it tough to know how to make pattern changes and rectify issues. Construction techniques and fabrication will also have an effect on the outcome of the final garment.

Students can best overcome these challenges by gleaning as much as possible from their technical staff on how to approach tasks. Producing multiple toiles will also mean they can catch problems before making the final garment. It is essential that they really look at their designs and attempt to create what they have drawn rather than what they think it should be. Taking photos during fittings and printing them the same size as their illustrations can help them see what they have produced as it brings the 3D back to 2D for comparison.

## What do you enjoy the most as a creative?

I enjoy working through the development of a concept into an idea and translating the idea into reality. I particularly enjoy working through challenges to come up with the most appropriate solution.

## What makes a successful garment?

Technically, a successful garment fits well and is comfortable to wear whilst being true to the design. The use of appropriate fabrics and the development of suitable finishes and construction techniques for those fabrics is key. It is essential to find the right balance between innovation and practicality. There are crucial details that mean the garment functions is wearable and can be related to by the wearer, which brings even the most extreme design back to something that people understand as fashion.

## Any advice for aspiring designers?

From a technical point of view, my advice would be that preparation is key. The actual construction of a garment can be quite quick as long as the patterns work, all fabrics and haberdashery are prepared correctly and all design details are finalized before the garment is produced. Don't start until you are ready to finish. Avoid changes during construction because these cost time and money. Whilst it is not essential to understand garment construction as well as an experienced technician, it is essential to be able to explain what the final outcome should be. The more information you can give, the more likely the outcome will be as you wish.

My advice would also be to take the time whilst studying to develop your ability to analyze the successful realisation of your designs into garments. Practicing with sampling, toiling and fitting will help you to gain an ability to compare your vision with what you are producing.

## Task

### The cocktail dress

The cocktail dress is a staple piece in any modern day wardrobe. This iconic dress is elegant and easy to wear, making it popular for many occasions. It is usually cut above the knee with a fitted bodice and some variation of volume in the skirt.

Your task is to design, pattern cut and sew this dress together. Your starting point is to research the style and incorporate techniques and methods that you have learned throughout the book.

**7.44 "Amour" and "Musette" Dior dresses.**

In your design, you should aim to include the following:

- Dart manipulation and introduction of style lines for fit and detail
- An area of volume—using ideas discussed in this chapter
- A combination of fabrics that can be both aesthetically pleasing and helpful with the overall silhouette

Once you have a design you want to create, start to think about your approach to pattern cutting. You might want to start from the blocks that you have created, or you might want to start draping on the stand. Either way you wish to create your idea, be playful and explore proportion and detail.

You should also consider the following while realizing your design:

- Which areas might need support? Does your design require a corset or internlining?
- The grain of your pieces. Is any part of your design cut on the bias, or does your fabric have a particular nap to it?
- Does this garment have any specialist fabrics that would need alternative or decorative seams?
- How can someone get into the garment?
- What are the appropriate fastenings?

**Tips for designing a cocktail dress**

Look at historical and contemporary references to help you in your design. You want to make sure the proportion of your dress is working and that you have considered the finer details of the garment. Pay close attention to the balance between the bust, waist and hem length of the dress. You might want to experiment with the position of the waistline to add a point of focus to the dress and raising or lowering the hemline.

**7.45 Mary Katrantzou SS16.**

# Finishes

This chapter will look at the "finishing touch." A garment can be faced, bound or left with a raw edge, depending on the desired look. Good knowledge of fastenings, linings, fabric behaviour, traditional techniques and specific fabric finishings is always necessary, as the look and feel of the finishes can make or break a garment. Some designers have created their own finishing techniques to give a unique look to their creations; for example, Levi's uses its back pocket stitching as a trademark.

**8.1 YMC SS16.**

# Linings

A lining can be added to a garment as an extra layer for several different purposes—to ensure that the shape of the garment is retained, for warmth or for design and comfort. It will also hide all the internal construction details. A lining can be worked in and can either cover the whole of the garment or act as a half lining. It can also be detachable as a zip-in or button-in version. Usually, jackets, coats, skirts and trousers are lined. The lining fabric can vary from silk and cotton to fur.

It is just as important to design the inside of a garment as the outside. Attention to detail is vital!

**8.2 Back view of a women's jacket by Ted Baker, shown inside out to expose the center back pleat in the lining for comfort.**

**8.3 Women's jacket by Ted Baker, shown inside out, to expose a lovely finish. Lining and front facing are sewn together with a pink binding in between. The inside chest pocket uses jets and a pink lining triangle to cover up the button (which fastens the inside pocket). This prevents the button from rubbing on the garment and damaging it.**

**8.4 Men's jacket by Ted Baker, shown inside out. A men's jacket offers more inside pockets than the women's. This particular jacket has a pocket for small change with a concealed zip on the bottom right side between the lining and facing. It also has a chest pocket for a wallet, a pocket for a mobile phone and additional spare pockets.**

**8.5 Women's trousers by Ted Baker, shown inside out to display the half lining from waist to knee.**

**8.6 Casual jacket by Joseph.**

**8.7 Joseph jacket shown inside out. It is half lined in the front, from shoulder to chest level. The sleeves are lined for comfort and this also makes it easier to slip into the jacket. The seams in the front and the pocket are bound for a neat finish.**

**8.8 The back of the Joseph jacket is completely lined.**

**8.9 This skirt lining hem has been finished with a lace trimming, showing attention to detail.**

## How to pattern cut a jacket lining

In most cases, linings have the same shape as the garment.

- When cutting the pattern for a jacket, the facings of the front are taken off the lining pattern.

- Some tailors add a small pleat at mid-armhole level on the lining front-piece, to accommodate the force that the lining pocket creates.

- At the hemline of the lining pattern, ⅜ in (1cm) is added to the finished hemline of the garment in order to create a pleat for extra comfort.

- The ease provided in the sleeve head is taken into a pleat or dart in the lining sleeve, as the lining fabric cannot be eased into the armhole as easily as the outer garment fabric.

- The lining needs to cover the bulk of the seam allowance inside a garment, so ⅜ in (1 cm) is added to the side seams of the body and sleeve.

- A pleat is added for comfort in the center back of the lining pattern.

- Sometimes a tough quality of lining is used for the sleeve (twill weave, for example), as there is a lot of movement and friction around the elbow area.

# Facings

A facing is used to finish a raw edge on a garment. It is mostly used when the edge is shaped, such as on a neckline. The facing is cut to the same shape as the edge line, stitched on and folded to the inner side. Facings are commonly added to areas such as the neckline, the armhole on a sleeveless garment, openings at the front and back or a hemline. Usually, the facing is cut in the same fabric as the garment and then lightly fused, but it can also be cut in a contrasting fabric or color to the garment.

**8.10 Dress by Joseph, shown inside out to display a faced neckline and armhole.**

**8.11 The gathered center part in the front neckline of the Joseph dress is turned into small darts at the facing.**

# Fastenings

Fastenings are functional items that will keep a garment closed. They can be hidden or made into a focal point. The family of fastenings is diverse, ranging from buttons, press studs, Velcro and magnets to buckles, hook-and-eye fastenings and zips. The choice of fastenings will dramatically influence the style of a garment. Avoid settling for your first idea, and have a good look at what the market has to offer.

8.12 Dress detail by Dolce & Gabbana, fastened in the center front with a hook-and-eye tape.

8.13 Hook-and-eye fastening on the neckline of a dress. It is placed at the end of the zip to hold the neckline in place.

8.14 Jacket and dress by Dolce & Gabbana. The jacket is fastened with large poppers.

8.15 Silk dress by Ted Baker, fastened with a rouleau loop and button, as well as a concealed zip in the left side seam.

8.16 Silk top by Hugo Boss, fastened in the center front by rouleau loops and covered buttons.

8.17 A dress with a concealed zip in the center back.

8.18 A printed top by Ted Baker, fastened on the neckline with a stitched tunnel and a decorative satin tie.

8.19 Jacket by Hugo Boss, fastened in the center front with bound buttonholes and covered buttons.

8.20 Detail shot of a bound buttonhole.

## The shirt

Traditionally, a shirt is closed by small buttons and buttonholes, although the buttons can come in different sizes. The buttonhole stand can be worked with visible or concealed buttonholes. Cuffs are also closed with a button and buttonhole.

**8.21–8.22 Detail showing a button stand with concealed buttonholes.**

## Trousers

For a casual look, use an elasticated waistband or a tunnel and cord. For a tailored solution, use a waistband with an underwrap, closing with a hook fastening or a button and buttonhole. The zip can be placed either in the center front or the side seam up to the waistband and covered from one side. Trouser waistbands are usually finished with belt loops to accommodate a belt.

**8.23–8.25 Different fastening options for trousers.**

## The skirt

Skirts can be fastened in various ways. When finished with a waistband, an underwrap can be created with a hook fastening or button and buttonhole. The zip opening (which reaches up to the waistband) would be sewn in, either concealed or with one or both sides covered.

If the zip is taken to the top of the waistline, use a small loop and button or a hook-and-eye fastening on the very top of the zip to ensure that it stays closed.

A skirt waistline can also be held in place by an elasticized waistband or a tunnel-and-cord finish. If you are seeking a different look, use a wrap closing, where the skirt is closed by one side wrapping over the other.

**8.26 Skirt shown inside out to display full lining.**  **8.27 The skirt has a tunnel-and-cord fastening.**

# Haberdashery

Fastenings and trimmings such as buttons, zips, elastics, studs and rivets are only some of the endless list of haberdashery. Haberdashery can be functional and/or decorative and will change with fashion. It can also make or spoil an outfit and control the fit of the garment.

Non-sew poppers or snap fasteners **(1)**

Skirt hook **(2)** This must be sewn on by hand

Popper or snap-fastener tape **(3)** This can be sewn on by machine.

Clips for braces **(4)**

Popper or snap fastener **(5)** This must be sewn on by hand.

Buckles and clips **(6)**

Brace clips **(7)**

Hook-and-eye fastenings **(8)** These must be sewn on by hand.

---

## Zips

It is important to choose the right zip for the garment being constructed. You can get zips with metal teeth, which are on a cotton or synthetic tape. These zips are strong and can be used for medium- to heavyweight fabrics. A lighter option is a synthetic polyester or nylon zip with plastic teeth, attached to a woven tape. An open-ended zip with either metal or plastic teeth can be used for jackets and coats. Concealed zips have plastic teeth and are easy to attach to garments.

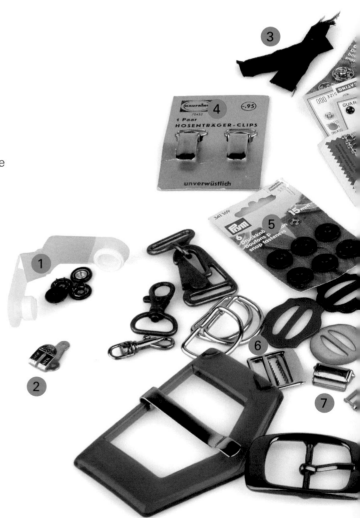

## Buttons and closures

Buttons are available in all kinds of materials such as glass, plastic, metal, leather, mother-of-pearl or covered with fabric. When sewing on a flat button with two to four holes, make sure to include the thread shank. It will be needed on most fabrics to give space for the underwrap (buttonhole layer) to lie flat beneath the fastened button. Closures, such as poppers and hooks, can be used as well as buttons. Here is just a selection of the variety of closures.

Pre-finished frog fastenings, one with a Chinese button and the other with a hook and loop attached **(9)**

Decorative zip puller to hook on to the zip head **(10)**

Hook-and-eye tape **(11)** This can be sewn on by machine.

Basic buckle that can be covered with fabric **(12)**

Sew-on leather coat hangers **(13)**

Non-sew hook and bar for skirt and trousers **(14)**

A selection of zips **(15)**

## Decorations and trimmings

Decorations such as beads, sequins, rosettes, bows and trimmings come in and out of fashion. Finding the right balance is not easy and sometimes less is more.

**Ready-made decorations** can be hand sewn or machine stitched on to the garment. Most of them are great fun for children's wear.

**Trimmings** for all kind of finishes are available in haberdashery shops. Some trimmings are elastic and can be used in lingerie and swimwear or as waistbands and cuffs on casual wear. Others are non-stretch like Petersham ribbon, woven jacquard ribbon, silken braids and piping.

**Lace trimmings** can be exposed or used in the underlayers of an outfit, for example on lingerie. The lace trimming can be manufactured in different ways.

**Embroidery** can be used to decorate a garment. It is time consuming but worthwhile. Many designers have the work done abroad, in order to keep the costs down. There is a vast choice of beads, sequins, pearls and bugle beads on the market, but do not forget that your creative eye might identify other materials that can be embroidered on to a garment.

1

Different kinds of decoration and trimmings, ready for application **(1)**

A selection of bugle beads, sequins, pearls and beads in different sizes **(2)**

A box of pearl beads, nylon thread and wire for attaching the beads **(3)**. When embroidering, use a slim hand sewing needle to make sure the needle fits through the hole of the bead.

Elasticated lace for lingerie **(4)**

Beaded lace edging is finished on both edges with a fine lace border and pearl bead decoration **(5)**

Netted lace whereby the base is netting **(6)**

Crocheted lace or broderie anglaise, which is an openwork, embroidered cotton trim that can be finished on one or both sides **(7)**

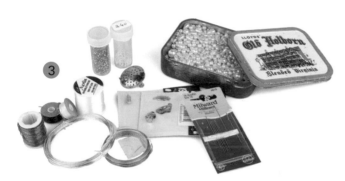

## Inspired practitioners
### Sheila McKain-Waid, Founder Laain/Creative Director Jaeger

Sheila is a womenswear designer, founder of active sportswear label LAAIN and Creative Director of Jaeger, where she is responsible for running the design team and leading the womenswear and accessories design, as well as being responsible for all creative and visual direction of the label. Sheila previously worked as a consultant for Donna Karan, before moving to Morgane Le Fay, Halson, and then Oscar de la Renta where she was Senior Designer. Before her post at Jaeger she was Head of Design at Daks.

**Where did you train?**
I first studied textile design at the University of Kansas and went on to study Fashion Design at the Fashion Institute of Technology in New York, USA.

**What is your approach to research?**
At Jaeger it always starts with a trip somewhere. I like to take my design team out of the office so we can clear our heads and have a chance to all align and turn our focus to absorbing new ideas. We visit museums, vintage markets, art galleries.

For Laain and on a personal level, it usually starts with art. I try to take a couple of days and spend it either going to exhibitions or in the library at the V&A. My business partner Tamara and I also like to look through great vintage sportswear in Camden Market, and I also find social media creeping into a lot of the research. We do a lot of idea sharing via Instagram and Pinterest and have a digital file of ideas. I tend to start with three or four ideas and then as I work through them narrow my focus.

Fabric is also paramount in this process, I think fabric often informs much of the final outcome and I tend to go to Premiere Vision each season.

**How important is the construction process in what you design?**
It is vitally important to everything I design. Just changing the shape of a sleeve can so dramatically alter the appearance of a garment. At Jaeger, it is a balance of silhouette, proportion and volume and at Laain the focus is on functionality and line.

## How important is the development process?

I find the development process critical. From the structure of any fabric to the way it is cut to the finishing and trims there are so many variables, and I often find my best designs are informed by the process. I remember one collection I did was completely created around a circular zipper I found.

## How much designing do you do using a 3D approach?

I start every design with a rough sketch, but what works on paper is often very different to what works on a body. I think the first toile or proto fitting is the most critical. It is a bit like sculpture: the first construction of any garment is just a starting point and then it is a matter of working through the idea once it is on the body. With Laain, I have also increasingly had to think about functionality. The positioning of seams and pockets takes on a very different importance when clothing is being worn for high impact sport.

## How do you approach the finish of your garments?

I usually trial finishes on small swatches of fabrics, sometimes we spend entire days doing this, just looking at ways to add interest in the finishing details. Recently, I have been trying to replicate some of the finishes we use in sportswear and bring these into ready-to-wear. There is so much innovation in this arena it feels very modern when applied on ready-to-wear.

## What advice would you give aspiring designers?

I think one of the things I have discovered over the years is not to be so wedded to an idea, that you cannot allow something else to emerge from the process. Allow yourself to play and don't be afraid to go in your own direction.

## Task

### Exploring haberdashery

- Compile samples of different zip finishings. Explore how to sew a concealed zip, trouser zip into a fly front, and an exposed zip as detail.
- Using hand stitching and machine techniques, find some trimmings that interest you. Experiment how these can be attached to garments or into seams.
- Practice sewing on sequins, beads and other trimming using hand sewing, and explore embroidery techniques.

**Exploring facings and linings**

- Design and pattern cut a simple garment that requires facings and linings. This could be a dress, a jacket or coat.
- Draft the facings into your pattern and review for placement and support. Analyze where the facings are and if they can be incorporated into the garment. For example, can the hem facings be turned up if on a straight edge? Do the facings need to be interlined for extra support?
- Once you have a draft of where the facings are, draft the lining for the rest of the garment. Remember the lining should be complementary to the garment and you should be aiming for a clean finish on the inside. Add extra pleats or girth to your lining for comfort if needed.
- Finally, cut the outer body of your garment out in self fabric, facings in self fabric (possibly fused) and the lining in appropriate fabric. When sewing, pay attention to the order of make; you will need to leave a section of lining open in the garment so you can "bag out" the piece when it is all attached. This opening is usually somewhere discreet, for example, in the sleeve for the hem of the lining.
- Once the garment is turned back through, hand or machine finish this opening closed. Press or steam well and review.

# Conclusion

This book has taken a journey through all the most important areas of garment construction, starting with the challenging skill of pattern cutting and moving on to the specialist areas of couture, tailoring and industrial methods, through to draping on the mannequin and a detailed examination of the various tools and techniques that can be employed. I hope that this will awaken your interest and encourage you to try out some exciting shapes on the pattern table and mannequin stand.

If you intend to develop your garment construction skills, it is a good idea to start a sample box for collecting all kinds of samples, such as interlinings, shoulder pads, tapes and so on. Make sure that you label your samples so that you know which shop you found them in. This will be very helpful and should, in the long run, save you time running around.

It is hoped that this book will encourage you to become more curious about garment construction and inspire you to start your own investigations. However, please remember one thing: learn the basics first, and then start experimenting. Always question what you are doing and why you are doing it.

**Batting** Tangled fiber sheets used in quilting and stuffing.

**Bespoke** Custom-made, one-off tailored garments.

**Block (also known as a sloper)** A 2D template, constructed using measurements taken from a size chart or an individual model. It has no style lines or seam allowance.

**Boning** Method for stiffening foundation garments, like bodices for dresses. The metal or plastic strips called bones were originally made from whalebone.

**Brassiere** An undergarment worn by women to mold and support the breasts. Now known as the bra.

**Breakline** The folding line of a collar.

**Breeches** Trousers worn by men until the late nineteenth century.

**Bustle** Nineteenth-century undergarment that supported back fullness in skirts, using pads, cushions or arrangement of steel springs attached below the waist at the back of a woman's dress.

**Canvas** A combination of hair and wool threads with horsehair twists or viscose filaments. Canvas is used for creating body and long-lasting shape in a garment.

**Calico** A cheap cotton fabric, available in different weights, used for making toiles.

**Classic** A garment that has a widespread acceptance over a period of time and is well known by name (such as the little black dress, for example).

**Course** The horizontal (crosswise) ridge of a knitted fabric.

**Crinoline** Stiff underskirt from the 1840s and 1850s. Stiffness was achieved using crinoline fabric, often combined with horsehair for extra rigidity.

**Darts** Darts control excess fabric to create shape on a garment when stitched together to a zero or pivotal point.

**Ease** An allowance added to a pattern in order to allow for extra comfort or movement.

**Elastomers** A synthetic material that has extensibility with complete elastic recovery.

**Facing** Used to finish a raw edge of a garment. Facings are mostly used when the edge is shaped; for example, on a neckline.

**Felting** The knotting together of fibers (using heat or friction and chemicals) to produce a matted material.

**Finishes** Processes and techniques that are used to manipulate the appearance, characteristics, performance or handle of a fabric. Also the way a garment is neatened during construction; for example, with seams and hems.

**Gathering** Two parallel loosely stitched rows that are pulled up to create fullness and a decorative, ruffled effect.

**Grain line** A grain line indicates the direction in which a pattern piece is laid onto fabric before being cut out.

**Girdle** Ladies' undergarment created in the 1930s in order to shape and hold the lower part of the female body, occasionally including the legs.

**Gauze** Loose-woven fabric made of loosely twisted cotton yarns. Garments are often given a crinkled finish and are worn unpressed.

**Grading** The increase or decrease of a pattern size.

**Godet** Panel of fabric inserted into a garment, such as a skirt or dress, to create flare.

**Gore** Fabric panels used in garment construction to add structure and flare.

**Haute couture** Garments made to measure for a specific customer.

**Holes and notches** These indicate where the separate pieces of fabric will be attached to one another.

**Hoops** A hoop-shaped structure made up of a series of round or oval circles (whalebone, wire, or cane) gradually increasing in size from top to bottom.

**Horsehair** Long, very coarse hair from the mane and tail of a horse, used in structural fabrics and wadding.

**House model** A male or female model with the body shape that a designer works towards.

**"Hourglass" figure**  A body shape or garment with a full bust, pinched-in waist and full, curving hips, representing the shape of an hourglass.

**Interlining/fusing**  This is a woven or non-woven fabric that is used between the lining and the outer fabric of a garment. It is either fusible (iron-on) or non-fusible (to be sewn-in).

**Knife pleats**  Pressed pleats that go in one direction.

**Lapel**  The decorative rever of a tailored jacket.

**Lining**  Fabric used on the inside of a garment to hide the construction. It extends the garment's life as it helps to retain the shape. It also makes the garment more comfortable to wear.

**Nap**  Fiber ends that stick out on the surface of the fabric, making it soft to the touch. These fabrics, such as velvet, corduroy, fur and brushed cotton, must be cut in one direction only.

**Netting**  Net is an open-mesh, transparent fabric. It can range from very sheer to stiff and heavy.

**Overlocking**  Quick and efficient way of stitching, trimming and edging fabrics in a single action to neaten seams.

**Pad stitching**  A pad stitch is used to join two layers of materials together, using a diagonal stitch that is staggered from one row to the next.

**Padding**  Extra bulk in a garment used to emphasize parts of the body as well as adding shape and support.

**Pattern**  Initially developed from a design sketch using a block. A designer or pattern cutter adapts the block to create a pattern that includes style lines, drapes, pleats, pockets and other adjustments.

**Petticoat**  Ladies' undergarment, firstly worn under the skirt (between the sixteenth and seventeenth centuries) and later worn visibly as an outer garment (between the seventeenth and eighteenth centuries).

**Pret-à-porter**  French term used in fashion design to describe ready-to-wear.

**Quilting**  Traditionally, quilting is made up of layers that are stitched together in a series of seam diagonals to form a diamond pattern. Quilting fabrics are available in two-layered and three-layered variations. The two-layered version has a top or face layer made of decorative fabric. The second layer is wadding, made out of cotton or synthetic fiber batting.

**Sample**  The first version of a garment made in the main fabric.

**Scye**  Technical name for the sleeve head.

**Seam allowance**  Seam allowance is added to seams to allow for stitching. These allowances vary depending on the kind of seam used and are usually facing the inside of a garment.

**Slash and spread**  A method used to add extra volume and flare.

**Stand**  A dressmaking mannequin or dummy.

**Superlock**  A very fine and tight overlocking stitch used on knit and jersey fabrics. It creates a wavy edge.

**Tanning**  A process for treating leather by removing the hair of the skin and revealing the grain.

**Tier**  Originating from the word *attire*, a tier is headwear made of gold and gems worn on pomp occasions since the fifteenth century.

**Toile**  The fabric sample used for fitting a garment. A toile has no finished seams, no fastenings such as buttonholes and buttons and no lining or facings.

**Top-stitch**  To stitch on the right side of the garment.

**Tricot**  Wrap-knit fabric made with two different yarns. It has fine wales on the front and crosswise ribs on the back.

**Trunk hose**  A short puffy trouser worn by men, with a pair of dense tights in the mid-sixteenth century.

**Underpressing**  The action whereby the iron is slipped between the hemming and outer fabric.

**Wales**  The vertical ridges in a knitted fabric.

**Welt**  The reinforced or decorative border of a garment or pocket.

# Bibliography

Aldrich W (2004) *Metric Pattern Cutting* WileyBlackwell

Amaden-Crawford C (2005) *The Art of Fashion Draping* Fairchild Publications, Inc.

Arnold J (1977) *Patterns of Fashion: Englishwomen's Dresses & Their Construction* Drama Publishers

Barbier M and Hanif-Boucher S (2005) *The Story of Lingerie* Parkstone Press Ltd.

Baudot F (1997) Paul Poiret (*Fashion Memoir*) Thames and Hudson

Burda (1988) *Burda perfekt selbstschneidern (Broschiert)* Burda Medien Vertrieb

Cabrera R and Flaherty Meyers P (1983) *Classic Tailoring Techniques: A Construction Guide for Men's Wear* Fairchild Books

Cabrera R and Flaherty Meyers P (1984) *Classic Tailoring Techniques: A Construction Guide for Women's Wear* Fairchild Books

Capucci R (1996) *Roberto Capucci al teatro farnese* Progretti museali

Chunman Lo D (2011) *Pattern Cutting* Laurence King

Cicolini A (2007) *The New English Dandy* Thames and Hudson

Cloake D (2000) *Lingerie Design on the Stand: Designs for Underwear & Nightwear* Batsford

Coates C (1997) *Designer Fact File* British Fashion Council

Creative Publ. Intl. (2005) *Tailoring: A Step-by-step Guide to Creating Beautiful Customised Garments* Apple Press

de Rethy E and Perreau J (1999) *Monsieur Dior et nous: 1947–1957* Anthese

Doyle R (1997) *Waisted Efforts: An Illustrated Guide to Corset Making* Sartorial Press Publications

Duburg A (2014) *Draping: Art and Craftmanship in Fashion Design* Artez Press

Hawkins D (1986) *Creative Cutting, Easy Ways to Design and Make Stylish Clothes* Everyman Ltd.

Hunnisett J (1991) *Period Costume for Stage and Screen: Patterns for Women's Dress: 1500–1800* Players Press

Jefferys C (2003) *The Complete Book of Sewing* DK Publishing

Jenkyn Jones S (2005) *Fashion Design* Laurence King Publishing

Joseph-Armstrong H (2005) *Pattern Making for Fashion Design* Pearson Education

Joseph-Armstrong H (2013) *Draping for Apparel Design* Fairchild

Jouve M-A (1997) *Balenciaga* Thames and Hudson

Kennett F (1985) *Secrets of the Couturiers* Orbis

Kirke B (1997) *Madeleine Vionnet* Chronicle Books

Langle E (2005) *Pierre Cardin: Fifty Years of Fashion and Design* Thames and Hudson

Major J and Teng Y (2003) *Yeohlee: Work, Material, Architecture* Peleus Press

Mankey C and Tortora P (2003) *Fairchild's Dictionary of Fashion* Fairchild Books

Martin R (1997) *Charles James* Thames and Hudson

Mendes V (2004) *Black in Fashion* V&A Publications

Sato H (2012) *Drape Drape* Laurence King

Shaeffer C (2001) *Couture Sewing Techniques* Taunton Press Inc.

Shaeffer C (2008) *Fabric Sewing Guide* Krause Publications

Sorger R and Udale J (2006) *The Fundamentals of Fashion Design* AVA Publishing

Taylor P and Shoben M (2004) *Grading for the Fashion Industry: The Theory and Practice* Shoben Fashion Media

Tomoko N (2007) *Pattern Magic*, Vol. 1 Laurence King

Tomoko N (2011) *Pattern Magic*, Vol. 2 Laurence King

Tomoko N (2012) *Pattern Magic: Stretch Fabrics* Laurence King

Wolff C (1996) *The Art of Manipulating Fabric* Krause Publications

# Museums and archives

**Bata Shoe Museum**
327 Bloor Street West
Toronto
Ontario
Canada M5S 1W7
www.batashoemuseum.ca

**Costume Gallery**
Los Angeles County Museum of Art
5905 Wilshire Boulevard
Los Angeles
CA 90036
USA
www.lacma.org

**Costume Institute, Metropolitan Museum of Art**
1000 5th Avenue at 82nd Street
New York
NY 10028-0198
USA
www.metmuseum.org

**Galeria del costume**
Amici di palazzo pitti
Piazza Pitti
1 50125 Firenze
Italy
www.polomuseale.firenze.it

**Kobe Fashion Museum**
Rokko Island
Kobe
Japan
www.fashionmuseum.or.jp

**Kyoto Costume Institute**
103, Shichi-jo Goshonouchi Minamimachi
Kyoto 600-8864
Japan
www.kci.or.jp

**MoMu**
Antwerp Fashion Modemuseum
Nationalestraat 28 2000
Antwerpen
Belgium
www.momu.be

**Musée de la mode et du costume**
10 avenue Pierre 1 er de serbie
75116 Paris
France
www.palaisgalliera.paris.fr/en

**Musée des Arts decoratifs**
Musee des Arts de la mode et du textile
107 rue de rivoli
75001 Paris
France
www.lesartsdecoratifs.fr/en/

**Musée des tissus et des arts decoratifs de Lyon**
34 rue de la charite
F-69002 Lyon
France
www.musee-des-tissus.com

**Museum at the Fashion Institute of Technology**
7th Avenue at 27th Street
New York
NY 10001-5992
USA
www.fitnyc.edu/museum

**Museum für Kunst und Gewerbe Hamburg**
Steintorplatz
20099 Hamburg
Germany
www.mkg-hamburg.de

**Museum of Costume**
Assembly Rooms Bennett Street
Bath, BA1 2QH
UK
www.museumofcostume.co.uk

**Museum of Fine Arts, Boston**
Avenue of the Arts
465 Huntington Avenue
Boston
Massachusetts 02115-5523
USA
www.mfa.org

**Museum Salvatore Ferragamo**
Palazzo Spini Feroni
Via Tornabuoni 2
Florence 50123
Italy
www.salvatoreferragamo.it

**Victoria and Albert Museum (V&A)**
Cromwell Road
South Kensington
London SW7 2RL
UK
www.vam.ac.uk

**Wien Museum**
Fashion collection with public library
(view by appointment)
A-1120 Vienna
Hetzendorfer
Strasse 79
Austria
www.wienmuseum.at

# Publications and magazines

*10*
*Another Magazine*
*Arena Homme+*
*Bloom*
*Collezioni*
*Dazed and Confused*
*Drapers Record*
*Elle*
*Elle Decoration*
*ID*
*In Style*
*International Textiles*
*Man About Town*
*Marie Claire*
*Marmalade*
*Numero Magazine*
*Oyster*
*Pop*
*Selvedge*
*Tank*
*Textile View*
*View on Colour*

*Viewpoint*
*Visionaire*
*Vogue*
*Wonderland*
*WWD Women's Wear Daily*

# Websites

www.britishfashioncouncil.co.uk
www.catwalking.com
www.costumes.org
www.fashion.about.com
www.fashion-era.com
www.fashionoffice.org
www.hintmag.com
www.infomat.com
www.londonfashionweek.co.uk
www.premierevision.fr
www.promostyl.com
www.showstudio.com
www.style.com
www.wgsn-edu.com

# Fashion forecasting

www.edelkoort.com
www.modeinfo.com
www.peclersparis.com
www.wgsn-edu.com

# Fashion trade shows

www.indigosalon.com
www.magiconline.com
www.pittimmagine.com
www.premierevision.fr
www.purewomenswear.co.uk

# Fashion employment agencies

www.denza.co.uk
www.smithandpye.com

# Index

# Acknowledgments and picture credits

## From Anette:

A big thank you to everyone who shared their knowledge, talent and time with me; the students of University College for the Creative Arts at Epsom; the students of Middlesex University; and the fashion team at Epsom, in particular Moira Owusu, Valentina Elizabeth and John Maclachlan.

Thank you to Peter Close for your help and advice and to Hannah Jordan for your technical drawings. Thank you also to Gary Kaye for your delightful illustrations, and the talented photographer James Stevens.

"Vielen Dank" Elena Logara-Pantel and Richard Sorger for your help and for being there for me. I would also like to thank the directors of Robert Ashworth Clothing for Men and Women in Reigate, Surrey; Elizabeth Long and Richard Clews for allowing the use of their collection for a photo shoot.

A big thank you to Martin Edwards, Robert James Curry, Tim Williams, Marios Schwab, Gemma Ainsworth, Linda Gorbeck, Peter Pilotto, Helen Manley, Clover Stones, Courtney McWilliams, Edina Ozary, Laurel Robinson, Chloe Belle Rees, Karin Gardkvist, Andrew Baker, Adrien Perry Roberts, Calum Mackenzie, Robert Nicolaas de Niet and Vincenza Galati.

Liebe Mama und Papa, danke dass Ihr mich bei meinem Treiben immer unterstuetzt habt. Ohne euch waere das alles nicht moeglich gawesen. Ich hab euch lieb.

## From Kiran:

Thank you to those who helped with their expertise, advice and beautiful work; the fashion team and students at Middlesex University, without whom this wouldn't be possible.

A particular special thanks to Richard Sorger, for your guidance and helpful words throughout.

Martine Rose and Lily Parker, thank you for everything.

A huge thank you to Thomas Tait, Rosie Armstrong, Sheila McKain-Waid, Robert Curry, Stuart McMillan, Izumi Harada, and Sharon Stokes and the team at Rapha. Your amazing and inspiring words are invaluable.

Mum, Dad, Pratima, Neesha, Pete and Nan. Thank you for being my rock. I love you all.

Lastly, my beautiful Spencer. I don't know where I would be without your unconditional love and support. Thanks for being there for me, always.

# Credits

Andrew Baker
Illustrations 1, 2, 3, 4 (p. 68)

Antoine Antoniol/Bloomberg via Getty Images
2.53

Antonio de Moraes Barros Filho/FilmMagic/
Getty Images
3.23, 7.2, 7.33

Antonio de Moraes Barros Filho/WireImage/
Getty Images
2.23, 4.23

Ben A. Pruchnie/Getty Images
2.11

Dan Kitwood/Getty Images
5.7

Derek Hudson/Getty Images
6.1

Dominique Charriau/WireImage/Getty Images
5.1

Gary Kaye www.garykayeillustration.com
1.3, 2.17a–f, 2.38, 7.38, 7.39, 7.40, 7.41, 7.42,
7.43
Illustrations x10 (unnumbered, pp. 142–143)
Images x7 (unnumbered, pp. 152–153)

Hannah Jordan and Amy Morgan
1.5–1.8, 2.3–2.9, 2.10 (technical drawings)
2.13, 2.16, 2.18–2.21, 2.24–2.26, 2.28, 2.30–
2.34, 2.36–2.39, 2.41, 2.43–2.46, 2.49–2.52,
2.54, 2.56, 2.58, 2.67–2.73
Layout of the pattern (pp. 58–59)
3.10–3.11, 3.14, 3.17, 3.19, 3.24, 3.25, 3.27,
3.29, 3.30, 3.32, 3.33, 3.37, 3.39, 3.40, 4.2,
4.3, 4.5, 4.8, 4.20, 4.21, 4.25, 7.27–7.32

Izumi Harada
Portrait, p. 62

James Stevens
Patterning cutting tools and equipment
(pp. 2–3)
1.2, 1.4, 2.10 (photograph), 2.12, 2.14, 2.27,
2.29, 2.40, 2.47, 2.55, 2.57, 2.59–2.63, 2.65,
2.74–2.76
Tools for the technique (pp. 66–67)
Photograph 5 (p. 68)
Photographs 6–7 (p. 68) copyright
J. Braithwaite & Co. (Sewing Machines Ltd)/
James Stevens
Photograph: 8 (p. 69)
Photographs 10–11 (p.69) copyright
J. Braithwaite & Co. (Sewing Machines Ltd)/
James Stevens
3.2–3.9, 3.12–3.13, 3.15, 3.16, 3.18,
3.20–3.22, 3.26, 3.28, 3.31, 3.34, 3.35, 3.36,
3.38, 3.41, 4.4, 4.16–4.18, 4.19 (Courtesy of
Courtney McWilliams), 4.24 (Courtesy of Yuki),
4.26–4.28, 5.8–5.11, 5.14, 5.15
Modeling tools and equipment (pp. 126–127)
6.2–6.5, 6.12–6.13
Supporting materials (pp. 144–145)
7.3, 7.4, 7.7, 7.8, 7.9–7.15, 7.16–7.17
(Courtesy of Caroline Gilbey), 7.18–7.24,
8.2–8.27 Haberdashery (pp. 182–185)

Jasmine Wickens
2.2

Jeff Spicer/Getty Images
7.5

© Josh Shinner
Portrait of Sheila McKain-Wald, p. 186

JP Yim/Getty Images
2.64

Keystone-France/Gamma-Keystone via Getty
Images
7.44

Keystone-France/Gamma-Keystone via Getty
Images
7.6

Kiran Gobin
1.9–1.11
4.29–4.31, 5.3–5.5, 5.12, 5.16, 6.10, 6.15,
6.20, 8.17

Liz McAulay/Getty Images
7.1

Loomis Dean/The LIFE Picture Collection/
Getty Images
2.66

MARTIN BUREAU/AFP/Getty Images
7.36

Martine Rose
Portrait, p. 14

MIGUEL MEDINA/AFP/Getty Images
2.1

Miles Willis/Getty Images
4.1

Pascal Le Segretain/Getty Images
2.15

Rob Curry
Portrait, p. 136

Rosie Armstrong
Portrait, p. 168

Sharon Stokes © 2016
Portrait, p. 84

Shelly Strazis/Getty Images
3.1

STAFF/AFP/Getty Images
5.2

Stuart McMillan
Portrait, p. 120

Thomas Tait
Portrait, p. 106

Tim Whitby/Getty Images
2.48

Tim Williams 6.6–6.11

Valentina Elizabeth
4.9–4.14

Victor Boyko/Getty Images
4.15, 6.14

Victor VIRGILE/Gamma-Rapho via Getty
Images
0.1, 0.2, 1.1, 2.22, 4.7, 4.22, 5.6, 5.13, 7.26,
7.45, 8.1

Vittorio Zunino Celotto/Getty Images
4.6

All reasonable attempts have been made to
trace, clear, and credit the copyright holders of
the images reproduced in this book. However,
if any credits have been inadvertently omitted,
the publisher will endeavor to incorporate
amendments in future editions.